FOOTBALL IS STILL A FUNNY GAME

Ian St-John and Jimmy Greaves

Edited by Bob Patience

Illustrations by Robin Bouttell

Copyright — Ian St John and Jimmy Greaves 1988

First published in 1988 by Stanley Paul & Co Ltd,
Brookmount House, 62–65 Chandos Place, Covent Garden
London WC2N 4NW

An imprint of Century Hutchinson Ltd

Century Hutchinson Australia (Pty) Ltd
88–91 Albion Street, Surry Hills, NSW 2010

Century Hutchinson New Zealand Limited
191 Archers Road, PO Box 40-086, Glenfield, Auckland 10

Century Hutchinson South Africa (Pty) Ltd
PO Box 337, Bergvlei 2012, South Africa

Set in Century Schoolbook by
Avocet Marketing Services, Bicester, Oxon.

Printed and bound in Great Britain by
Scotprint Ltd, Musselburgh, Scotland

British Library Cataloguing in Publication Data

St. John, Ian
Football is still a funny game: according
to Saint and Greavsie.
1. Association football
I. Title II. Greaves, Jimmy, *1940–*
III. Patience, Bob

ISBN 0 09 173737 0

Photograph acknowledgements

The authors and publishers would like to thank the
following for allowing use of copyright photographs:

AllSport: Celtic team, p.4; FA Cup final, p.4;
England v Ireland, p.4; Marco van Basten, p.17;
Rijkaard, Lineker and Beardsley, p.17; Bobby
Robson, p.18; Gary Lineker, p.19; Bobby Robson,
p.21; Copacabana kids, p.23; Brian Clough, p.45;
Nigel Clough, p.47; Chettle and John Barnes, p.49;
Cyrille Regis, p.51; Tommy Docherty, p.61; Roy
Aitken and Mixu Paatelainen, p.82; Ron Atkinson,
p.90; Norman Whiteside, p.92; Terry Venables and
Diego Maradona, p.101; Graeme Souness, p.105

Colorsport: Bill Shankly, p.8 (two pictures); Ron
Yeats, p. 10; Tommy Smith, p.13; Bryan Douglas,
p.26; Jack Charlton, p.28; Gordon West, p.31; Gordon
Banks, p.32; Denis Law, p.32/33; George Best, p.33;
Johan Cruyff, p.35; Ferenc Puskas, p.37; Ian St
John, p.38; Jim Baxter, p.39; Bob Paisley, p.41; John
Aldridge, p. 49; Dave Beasant, p. 52/53; Alan
Ashman, p.54; Jimmy Hagan, p.54; Tommy
Docherty, p.56; Tom Finney, p.58/59; Jimmy
Greaves, p.62; Peter Osgood, p.66/67; Pat Bonner
and Peter Beardsley, p.71; Terry McDermott, p. 78;
Roy Aitken and Billy McNeill, p.83; Willie Ormond,
p.85; Joe Jordan, p.86; Karl Heinz Rummenigge,
p.94; Frank McLintock, p.97; George Graham; p.98;
Joe Mercer, p.98; Bobby Campbell, p.103; Billy
McNeill and Tommy Craig, p.105; Alan Ball, p.107;
Jimmy Tarbuck, p.112

LWT: Ian and Jimmy, p.4

Press Association: Best, Osgood and Hudson, p.108

Sport and General: Johnny Haynes, p.26; Bobby
Robson and Don Howe, p.71

Sporting Pictures (UK) Ltd: Paul Gascoigne, p.22;
Wimbledon with the FA Cup, p.52/53; Ruud Gullit,
p.71; Ronnie Moran, p.73; Kenny Dalglish, p.74; Ian
Rush, p.76; Alex Ferguson, p.101; Alan Ball, p.105

Syndication International: Russ Abbott, p.127

Bob Thomas: Football League v Rest of the World,
p.105

And special thanks are due to Barry Roberts for
'Saint and Greavsie in Chilly Jockoland' (between
pages 64 and 65)

 CONTENTS

1 · SHANKS – FROM THE MEMORY 5

Saint and Friends

2 · A TOUCH OF THE INTERNATIONALS 17

Greavsie

3 · CHARACTERS 30

Saint

4 · MIRTH FROM THE MIDLANDS 44

Greavsie

5 · A VISIT FROM THE DOC 56

Tommy Docherty

6 · A DISH OF SCOUSE 70

Saint

7 · A DROP OF SCOTCH 81

Greavsie

8 · MANAGERS AND PLAYERS 90

Ian and Jimmy

9 · THE SHOWBIZ CONNECTION 113

Ian and Jimmy

Celtic beat Dundee United 2-1 to win the Scottish Cup and clinch the double in their centenary year *(top right)*, while lowly Wimbledon triumphed over mighty Liverpool in the FA Cup at Wembley. Lawrie Sanchez scores the winning goal *(above)*. And *(right)* underdogs Ireland nearly made it to the last four in the European Championships, beating England 1-0 on the way

1 SHANKS—FROM THE MEMORY

In the swinging sixties Bill Shankly was the uncrowned king of Liverpool. A bristle-headed Scot whose deep love of football laid the foundations of the great Liverpool FC of today. Shanks was in life a folk hero. In death a legend... and not just because of his football genius. For Shanks made things happen... and things happened to Shanks. His stories like the man are legend, and, in this opening chapter, three of his favourite sons, Ian St John, Ron Yeats and Tommy Smith, all part of the Shankly success story, remember the fun of being close to one of football's greatest.

First up, the Saint himself.

Saint

Anyone who has read *Football Is A Funny Game* will already be well aware that Bill Shankly not unnaturally had the biggest influence on my soccer career.

All of you who have not read the first tome ... go and buy it ... for I'm certainly not repeating the skullduggery and magic that my old guv'nor weaved to coax me away from Motherwell in 1960 for the then princely sum of £37,500. Suffice to say that he got me away from my home town just in time, for I was already making headlines ... and not of the right kind.

One night my young wife Betsy arrived home to announce, 'I've just seen something about Scotland's centre-forward being sacked ... I wonder who that could be?'

She nearly fainted when she found it was me the newspapers were headlining. As a young steelworks apprentice at the Bridge Works in Motherwell I had been caught with several others hopping the wall ... and the sack seemed inevitable. That meant that as a young married couple we would have to do without the £6 per week I earned at the time. Tragedy loomed, but then in stepped Bill Shankly with an offer of £30 per week and the chance to join a team of superstars ... his words.

To say he lit up my life brighter than the giant furnace which used to illuminate the Bridge Works is no understatement. He whisked me away to Anfield as part of his master plan to make Liverpool 'a bastion of invincibility' – again his words – and into a different world of great football, great friendship and great fun.

For Shanks nothing was too good for his boys. He had this philosophy. Players shouldn't worry about club matters ... they were the gladiators ... just concentrate on their fitness. And food was ultra-important.

Because of Shanks's harsh upbringing in the coalfields of Ayrshire he insisted on us eating well. To Shanks that meant steaks, steaks and more steaks. I don't suppose he had many opportunities to eat steak in the little mining village of Glenbuck where he hailed from ... so when he made the big time, there could be no other diet.

Twice a week on Fridays and Saturdays we had tomato soup, steak, chips and peas, followed by fresh fruit and cream ... lovely grub. Although it did become a wee bit boring, no-one dared tell the boss. Sometimes though the cheeky ones would comment: 'What are we having today boss? Steak and chips for a change?' It was water off a duck's back. And I can tell you it was years after I retired from the game before I could face steak again.

Mind you, Shanks's steak policy worked well enough until a number of Roman Catholics joined the team... that meant they had to have fish on Fridays. So suddenly the order became six steak and five fish dinners.

All worked well until Alfie Arrowsmith joined the team. Now, Alfie was a bit of a trencherman ... he would eat anything and on most occasions did. Trouble was ... he would eat the first meal he saw on the table, be it steak or fish. Suddenly players were not getting the meal they ordered and all manner of arguments would follow ... which always left Shanks more steamed up than the fish!

One night we were all sitting at dinner when in he roared: 'Arrowsmith – what kind of man do you call yourself when you don't know whether you're a steak or a fish?'

Food spluttered everywhere. Only Shanks would have ignored the terms Catholic or Protestant ... to him it was all about his food routine being upset!

Shanks was never one to mince words... nor speak them softly. In fact he was so loud that at times it was downright embarrassing. Outspoken he certainly was, and we often said that when the boss roared at Anfield you could hear him at Lime Street!

And he was not a man to be trifled with. He liked his own way and made sure he got it in towns and cities all over Europe and beyond.

Many a kitchen chef was transfixed when confronted by Shankly, his rasping voice demanding an answer to why his lads' meals were not on the table at precisely the time he had ordered. I don't remember too many meals being late after that kind of Shankly outburst.

I remember once playing in Rumania. We had a pleasant hotel and were relaxing in the bar when a couple of the lads asked for Cokes. Shanks jumped to his feet and demanded that the waiter bring some. The waiter, somewhat foolishly I thought at the time, said 'No Cokes.'

'No Cokes,' thundered Shanks. 'When my lads ask for Cokes they get Cokes.' And he stormed into the kitchen with the unfortunate waiter in tow. Minutes later he reappeared dragging a crate of Cokes and rounding on the unfortunate brother he stormed: 'You – you're a liar – and I'm not leaving it at that. I'm reporting you to the Kremlin!' And he meant it too.

Bill was also a strict disciplinarian. He'd spend many an anxious hour outside the team's hotel waiting for players to return from a quiet drink after a match abroad. And woe betide those who turned up late for curfew... which was usually around eleven o'clock.

On one foreign trip a group of us merrily returning to the hotel were met by a frightening sight... the boss, hands on hips in best Cagney style, waiting for us in the main street.

Lights went on all over the village square as he roasted us from a few hundred yards range.

'St John - you're a disgrace to the Red of Liverpool.'

'Smith - you're an eighteen-year-old hooligan!'

'Yeats - how can you lead on the football field when you can't get the lads back to the hotel on time?'

Then he noticed his favourite ... Ian Callaghan ... the brilliant little winger we christened the 'Choirboy' because Shanks could not see any wrong in him.

Realising he would have to chastise Cally too Shanks could only splutter: 'And as for you Callaghan ... I'm going to tell your missus you were out until midnight.'

Shanks would always wait up no matter how late it was just to catch any miscreant, and for two players that proved a painful experience.

We had played Anderlecht, the famous Belgian side, in the European Cup, and a couple of the lads outstayed their welcome at the local casino. It was around 2 a.m. when they reached the hotel, and suspecting everyone would be asleep they were horrified on turning a corner to see Shanks seated in a chair at the end of their corridor. There being no way of passing Shanks unnoticed they decided discretion was the better part of valour and parked themselves in a linen cupboard, where they slept until 5.30 a.m.

Stiff and sore they made their way to their rooms, only to find Shanks sitting in the same chair near their doors.

Shanks woke with a start and asked: 'Now lads - where would you be off to?'

Quick as a flash the lads countered: 'Couldn't sleep boss - so we're off for an early morning walk.'

'Good idea,' replied Shanks. 'It'll do you good. But make sure you're back in time for breakfast.'

Exit the lads... back to the linen cupboard for two more uncomfortable hours.

Shanks was also fiercely patriotic and he refused to act any differently abroad from the way he did at home. In fact when we toured America he refused to change his watch.

He would prepare for bed at 6 p.m. at night... 'I'm just off to bed lads,' he would say.

'But boss it's only six at night,' we'd reply.

'No lads,' Shanks would respond. 'We may be in America and it may be six o'clock here, but the proper time is on my watch and I'm off to bed.'

This eccentricity caused untold havoc. By the time the lads were sneaking back to the hotel in the early hours of the morning Shanks would be up and about looking for his breakfast and someone to talk to. We avoided him like the plague!

There were three things Shanks wanted to see in America: Jack Dempsey's Bar (the ex-Heavyweight Champ was one of Bill's great heroes); Al Capone's car; and Boot Hill.

He viewed the first two, and then whilst in New York he jumped into a yellow cab demanding 'Take me to Boot Hill.' It must have been the first time ever a New York cabbie was speechless. He hadn't a clue what Shanks was on about, and after a few minutes he asked him where Boot Hill was.

Shanks, brought up on a diet of Tom Mix, Roy Rogers and John Wayne movies, was astounded: 'You don't know your way to Boot Hill man? That's ridiculous ... every town in America's got a Boot Hill!'

Bill was a very proud man. He would hear

Above: Shankly the inimitable – 'Carry on the praise lads – I deserve it!'

Left: Koppites paying homage to the King – 1974 Charity Shield

no criticism of his team ... even from the most lofty of directors.

In the early days his manager's office was opposite the directors' box and from it he once heard Mr Cecil Moores, head of the Littlewoods Pools empire, criticising Tommy Leishman, an excellent little player.

After the match Shanks stormed into the reception and shouted: 'There's a man out there saying Tommy Leishman not only should have been substituted but shouldn't have been playing at all. Any man making such stupid comments has no right to even watch Liverpool.' At that moment Mr Moores entered the room and Shanks having no idea who he was shouted for all to hear ... 'And that's the stupid ****er I'm talking

about!' That he survived to become a legend after that says something for his genius.

Shanks was always immensely proud of his staff and the fact that we were always first to have all the new physio equipment around ... and to be fair he sometimes got rather carried away with it all.

He was also proud of Bob Paisley's expertise as a physiotherapist. Especially as Bob had just taken delivery of a new electronic treatment machine. One morning Bob was busy treating an injury when he heard Shanks's voice from outside. Shanks was talking to someone saying 'Don't worry son, this man has the expertise to cure anything. And with our new machinery we can work miracles.'

8

The door opened and in walked Shanks accompanied by a man in a wheelchair who'd been in it, incidentally, for three years! Shanks said, 'Well Bob, what can you do for our friend here?'

Bob took one look and said, 'Well Bill, if you put him in my car I'll run him down to Lourdes.'

Ian Callaghan was an early victim of the machine. He'd been unable to go to the toilet for about a week. Shanks brought him to Bob and said, 'We'll soon cure that.'

Bob attached a few wires to Cally, I won't say where, but they had the desired effect. Cally missed the next four training sessions and lost about two stone in weight in the process!

Another example of Shanks's pride was the time he signed Tony Hateley. He strode onto the pitch with the crowd chanting his name, walked to the Kop, held his arms out and said 'Carry on, I deserve it.'

At our training ground, Melwood, we kept a pitch for special occasions. No-one was ever allowed to train on it. When Inter Milan came over for a European Cup match they were actually allowed to train on it, and the Italians were the only people ever allowed to do so. They had a great player called Del Sol. Shanks was so proud of his new turf that he came to me after they'd finished training and said, 'You know what Del Sol told me? He said ours was the greenest grass he'd ever seen!'

That was how proud Shanks was. He once said 'If I were a street cleaner I'd have the cleanest street in the country!' Whatever he had done he would have had pride in it.

Bill could rant and rave with the best of them, and sometimes his language was choice, but he was a great man for his players ... particularly the special ones, for whom he could always find an excuse for any wrong doing. We knew it at Anfield and took advantage at times ... but it was a reputation that had followed him from his time at Huddersfield Town.

When Shanks was manager at Huddersfield he had a young lad called Denis Law. Denis didn't show up for pre-season training and Shanks was fuming. He called for the trainer and told him to pretend he was Denis Law. He was to knock on the door and enter when called. The trainer duly did this and Shanks tore into him.

'You, Law, can't be bothered to turn up for training. Who do you think you are! Everyone else can turn up but not you. You're finished. On the next train back to Scotland ... no, no, hang on we'll start again.'

So the trainer dutifully went out, and as he was waiting along came Denis Law. He told Denis he was in big trouble. Shanks shouted for the trainer to enter, but instead in went Denis. Shanks looked at him and said, 'Denis, hello son. Would you like a cup of tea? We've been wondering where you were.'

That was typical Shankly ... he loved stars and Denis was amongst the first he discovered. I'll never forget the man. His style and self-assurance plus the million laughs we had with him will never leave me ... nor will the memories of the great days on the field with the team that Shankly built. Looking back he didn't build a team, he built an empire.

═══════ o ═══════

Ron Yeats was captain of Shanks's team in the sixties. Signed from Dundee United for £30,000 big Ron was the cornerstone of Liverpool's defence. When he was signed Shanks described him to the press as 'a Colossus ... come and see this lad ... walk around him if you want.'

Shanks was so proud of his signing he bragged to Everton boss Harry Catterick: 'With Ron Yeats at centre half we could play Arthur Askey in goal!'

Ron, like Saint, shared in the great days with Shanks and the memories are still vivid.

Ron Yeats

During a bad winter we went to play a night game at Coventry. Shanks was a very canny man and noticed, when we arrived, that although the pitch had been frozen, it had also thawed down one side due to a brief spell of sunshine.

He pulled me to one side and asked if I thought it a good idea for the referee to toss up before the game. In doing this we'd know which way we were kicking and the wingers could adjust their boots accordingly. The one playing on the soft side could wear studs while the other could have a smooth sole.

I agreed, and so did referee Finney, who was a top international referee of the time.

Ron Yeats – cornerstone of the Liverpool defence in the Sixties

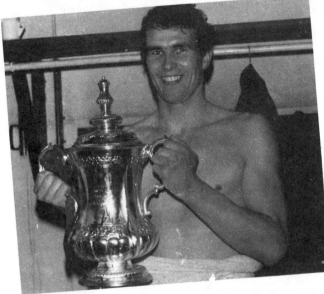

We went to the referee's room about half an hour before kick-off for the coin to be tossed. We were joined by Gordon Milne, who was an ex-Liverpool player, and George Curtis, now general manager of Coventry, who was the captain.

The referee tossed the coin; I shouted tails and won. Shanks put his arm round me and said, 'Well done, son.' He then proceeded to leave the room.

Gordon Milne said, 'Hang on. Aren't you going to tell us which way you're kicking?'

Shanks was obviously embarrassed at being caught out and said. 'Oh ... aye, of course. You tell him Ron.' And left.

I couldn't stop laughing at the thought of Shanks's unwillingness to share his secret with the opposition, not to mention his advantage. Afterwards, quite surprised that anyone had caught on, he said to me, 'That Gordon Milne, watch out for him. He's a sharp character.'

During the close season at Anfield, the first team would go off on their summer holidays, but not Shanks. He lived not only for the club but also for his five-a-side training games.

The playing of his beloved five-a-side games, which he would never allow to end until his team were in the lead, was still possible due to the apprentices training throughout the summer.

On one particular day he was appalled to find himself at the training ground with only nine players. Short of going out and dragging someone in off the street, he was at a complete loss. He scoured the ground and changing rooms in a faint hope of finding a player, but this proved fruitless.

Shanks stood on the edge of the pitch scratching his head when the local milkman drove up in his float. Shanks made a beeline for him, passed the time of day, then asked,

'You don't by any chance fancy a game of five-a-side?'

The milkman said, 'Bill, you know I'd do anything for you, but I'm 59 and never kicked a ball in my life.'

Shanks replied, 'You won't have to kick a ball. You'll be in the opposition.'

One aspect of the game during my time as captain which differed from the modern game was the rule about using a coin to decide a drawn game. This, on reflection,

was quite ludicrous when you consider that over three hours of European football could be decided on the toss of a coin.

The first time it happened to us was during a match against FC Cologne. We'd drawn a game at Cologne, another at Anfield, and a third at a neutral ground in Brussels.

The referee then reached in his pocket and pulled out a coin. Neither side wanted a result this way, but those were the rules. Luckily for us it had been a wet night, and

11

when the coin landed it stuck end up in the mud. Then, to my horror, it slowly began to fall over in favour of the opposition. I quickly jumped in and protested to the referee, asking for the coin to be tossed again.

The referee agreed, but not the Cologne players, who went berserk at my request. The coin was duly tossed for the second time and we went through to the next stage of the European Cup.

Shanks was delighted but, unfortunately, the second time it happened to us we were not so lucky. It was after a game against Bilbao and again we had three drawn games.

This time the referee produced a plastic disc coloured red on one side and white on the other. Seeing as they were the teams' respective colours I had no call to make. The disc landed white side up, Bilbao's colours, and we lost.

I came into the dressing room and Shanks said, 'Well son, you won us the last game on a coin but lost out on this one.'

I said, 'No Boss, it wasn't a coin. It was a plastic disc. Red and white.'

Shanks then asked me which side I'd picked. I told him I didn't have any choice seeing as we were playing in red!

Shanks replied, 'No son, for all we know you could have called white. I've a good mind to lodge a complaint!'

That was Shanks. He could never accept defeat, especially on the toss of a plastic disc.

During our successful years in the sixties we went to America having won the FA Cup.

New York was the place where Shanks decided to hold a press conference in a hotel lounge. I was sat having a quiet drink with the Saint, and Shanks was opposite with Bob Paisley and the trainer Reuben Bennett. Also present were about forty or fifty American reporters.

Football was in its infancy in the States at this time, and one reporter asked Shanks who was the best player he'd ever seen. Shanks's reply was not only the best player he'd ever seen, but one he'd actually played alongside. It was, of course, the great man, Tom Finney.

The reporter then asked who Tom Finney was. The Saint and I almost choked on our drinks, knowing full well what Shanks's reaction would be. Shanks went red in the face and exploded. 'You mean to tell me you've never heard of the great Tom Finney?' he roared. 'That's it, the conference is over! If you don't know who Tom Finney is then you know nothing about football! And another thing, with people like you around, this game will never catch on over here!'

He then stormed out leaving a bewildered group of pressmen wondering what on earth they'd said.

But that was Shanks - dramatic to the extreme. He was a one off. A miracle man. Some might say he was too wrapped up in Liverpool, but I can't take that. He recognised great talent, and his love of football burned deeper than any other man I have ever known. There will never be another like him.

═══════ O ═══════

Eventually, behind Ron Yeats and Saint in that Liverpool team of Shankly's, a new name appeared... that of Tommy Smith. Tommy, say Liverpool fans, wasn't born... he was quarried. It wasn't long before young Tommy acquired something of a hard man image ... something he disagrees with. He'll agree to having been a hard tackler, a hard worker who gave one hundred and fifty per cent. A true professional ... but having said that, a hard one.

One thing he'll agree wholeheartedly

about ... being one of Shankly's boys was an experience he'll never forget ... both on and off the field!

Tommy Smith

I pulled a thigh muscle in a cup game against Tottenham - this was the year we were beaten by West Brom after a third replay. I had missed the first two games due to a leg injury, so I was eager to get fit for the third.

The prescribed treatment was to shave the affected leg around the muscle and strap it up tightly. Joe Fagan decided that an extra long pair of shorts was required to disguise my injury because Bill Shankly didn't like anyone to show a weakness. This, of course, was done without the knowledge of Shanks. Joe was in the process of shaving my leg when Shanks entered and demanded to know what was going on. Joe explained and Shanks immediately took him to task saying that no player of his was taking the field with a strapped leg.

After listening to the argument for some minutes, I said, 'Hang on Boss, it's my leg you're discussing here.'

To which Shanks replied, 'No son. It's not your leg, it's not my leg, it's Liverpool's leg!' That was a measure of the dedication the man had for his club.

The upshot of this was that I played in the game and we were eventually beaten 2-1.

Tommy Smith ... just frightening!

But had I not played, I would not have found myself in the trouble that followed.

During the match, with about ten minutes to go, the ball went out of play. I rushed across to take the throw, intent on getting the game moving as quickly as possible, and shouted to Chris Lawler to get the ball across. The throw was taken, the game ended, and we retired to the dressing room somewhat downhearted.

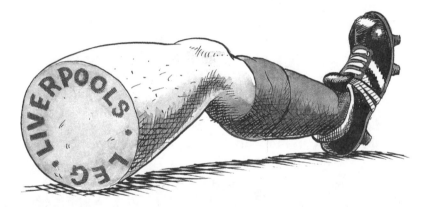

A young lad who was looking after the kit entered the dressing room and said there was a policeman outside wanting a word with me. At the time I thought it was a cousin of mine who was in the police force and told the lad to tell him I'd be out shortly. The lad left, only to return a few seconds later. He said, 'It's not your cousin, and he's still waiting.'

By this time I'd changed so I went to see what the problem was. I was greeted by the sight of a young bobby, helmet under his arm, propping up a push bike.

He said, 'Am I right to assume you were number four on the pitch tonight?' I answered yes. He then added, 'And according to the programme your name is Smith?' I told him it was. He then said, 'Right, I'm cautioning you that anything you may say will be taken down,' and he proceeded to give me a full caution. Needless to say I was at a loss for words. Eventually I asked what it was all about and he said, 'At two minutes past nine you were heard to say to a fellow player "Give me the ****ing ball".'

I immediately thought it was a joke and said, 'If you'd heard what was said after the second goal went in you'd be locking up eleven players, a manager and twenty thousand supporters!' He told me he wasn't joking and proceeded to write my comments down in his notebook.

It was then that Bill Shankly intervened. He strode across and in his usual style asked, 'What's the matter, son?' I told him what the policeman had said and that I was being charged with using foul and abusive language in a public place. Shanks couldn't believe it either.

'Come on son, you're not telling me that my boy here was being offensive?'

The policeman once again related his story, to which Shanks turned on him with much arm waving, and slipping into his native Scots accent left the young officer completely dumbfounded. Then he added, 'And my advice to you is to **** off quick before I let the tyres down on your bike.'

Luckily for all concerned, Joe Mercer happened along and sorted out the mess. I apologised to the policeman, only to find out later that he made a habit of this and had booked Mike Summerbee a couple of weeks before for the same offence.

I've been accused of intimidating people on the field, but at one particular game at Norwich I was guilty of frightening the life out of a supporter on the terraces.

I'd suffered a leg injury and had to leave the pitch. Ronnie Moran came across to help me round to the other side of the ground where the players' tunnel was. Being away from home I was receiving the usual abuse from the Norwich supporters and informed Ronnie that it was time I got my own back. Ronnie was puzzled at this, but was soon to realise, and share, the joke. As we passed the main bulk of opposition supporters, one in particular was hanging over the low wall calling me for all he was worth. At this stage I'd better point out that having lost my front teeth some years earlier, I had false ones fitted, but always removed them before a game. I suppose this made me look even more aggressive, if not uglier. As we passed the supporter in question, I spread my arms wide, placed my nose within half an inch of his, and let out an almighty growl! The poor bloke leapt about ten feet backwards, almost landing in the stands.

I had a second experience with crowds soon after, but on this occasion it involved my home fans. The time was the late sixties and Liverpool had experienced a bad year. Second in the league, semi-finals of the cup, but, for Liverpool, a bad year.

Every week the same supporter in a certain section of the crowd would have a go at me. Not having time to search the crowd I couldn't pinpoint the offender. During one game towards the end of the season he was in good form, accusing me of everything from drinking too much to losing Liverpool the title.

The game was played on a beautiful sunny day. The ball went out of play, and also coincided with an injury, and the game was stopped. I then found myself behind the goal retrieving the ball accompanied by yet another onslaught. I also found myself with time to search the crowd for the familiar voice, but to no avail. In desperation I shouted, 'All right, who is it?'

Suddenly, as if Moses had waved a stick, the crowd parted to reveal a solitary supporter. All fingers pointed at the guilty party and what must have been a hundred voices shouted in unison, 'It was him!'

This poor bloke had received the final humiliation, especially after I explained that I'd be waiting for him outside the players' entrance after the match. If the ground could have opened up I'm sure he'd have been only too glad to disappear from the face of the terraces.

During a match against Coventry, which was a morning game because of the Grand National, I found myself marking a player called Tommy Hutchinson. Usually Tommy was a talented player who could run rings round defenders, but on this occasion he was having a bad game. As he'd already been chosen to play for Scotland I decided to psych him out. I uttered comments like 'How can you be playing for Scotland when you can't get the ball past an old-timer like me?' Which did nothing for Tommy's confidence.

Liverpool were awarded a penalty and Alec Lindsay, who never missed, strode up

and hammered the ball into the net.

Tommy accused Alec of being lucky and in a vain attempt to save face said to me, 'Tell you what, I'll bet you a hundred pounds you can't beat me in a race back to the halfway line.'

I replied, 'Right, you're on. But only if we have another bet of two hundred pounds that when we get there we'll have a fight and I'll win!'

Needless to say Tommy didn't take up the offer and strode off still muttering how lucky we were.

I have, on occasions, been the victim of violence. I remember one game we played against Spurs. As usual at White Hart Lane, I'd gone out to inspect the pitch. Or should I

15

say sand – it was like Blackpool beach in those days. I was strolling around deciding whether to wear boots or sandals when suddenly a house brick flew over my head and landed a foot away. Obviously someone had taken offence at my reputation. In fact, when I saw it coming I didn't know whether to let it land or head it back!

Another time I was a victim of violence from my own team-mate! I was fifteen and playing five-a-side against possibly the hardest man to play the game – Gerry Byrne, the Liverpool full back. I had the ball and jiggled it past Gerry. The next thing I remember was a crack and then waking up requiring a number of stitches over my eye. I came off feeling sorry for myself to be greeted by Shanks for what I thought would be a sympathetic word. He just winked, laughed to himself and said, 'That'll teach you to sidestep Gerry Byrne!'

In fact, Gerry was the only Liverpool player who was banned from tackling in the Friday practice game. Shanks actually insisted on this to protect his other players.

A favourite Shanks story involves the time I was captain. Shanks took me to one side and told me that the wages required re-structuring and would I have a word with the lads.

The next Monday I found myself walking round Melwood, our training ground, with Shanks. I explained what the lads wanted in bonuses for a win, draw, etc., and Shanks said, 'Oh no, we can't have that.'

So I went back to the lads, had another discussion, and found myself once again strolling round Melwood with the Boss. I explained the feelings of the other players over bonuses and Shanks rounded on me!

'You Smith,' he said, 'you'd cause trouble in a cemetery! You're always stirring things up around here!'

By this time I was totally confused. After all, it was Shanks who'd asked me to discuss it with the lads in the first place!

The next week Shanks invited me to walk with him yet again and I reluctantly followed. He calmly announced that he'd considered the players' requests and they were fine. It was only later that I discovered that Shanks had to have his say, his own little argument. After that he was all right. I just happened to be the captain and so became the foil for this mild form of bartering.

One perk we had at Liverpool was a low-interest loan facility. Anyone wishing to buy a house could approach the club for a mortgage. I had decided on a new house, but, as the value was high, I didn't approach Shanks. Instead, I went to the club secretary requesting a £20,000 loan. This was being considered when I bumped into Shanks. He was livid.

'You know, Tommy,' he said, 'John Toshack has just been in and asked me for a loan of ten thousand pounds to buy a house! Ten thousand pounds! Good God man, you could buy three houses in my road for that!'

I suppose you could when Shanks bought his house some years ago, but it wasn't an excessive request by that time.

'And there's something else,' he added. 'Some bugger's just been in to Peter Robinson and asked for twenty thousand!'

I didn't have the courage to tell him it was me so I just muttered my disapproval and quickly left.

That was one tackle I really didn't fancy!

2 A TOUCH OF THE INTERNATIONALS

O.K., before any of you start, so I got it wrong again – England didn't win the European Championship like I exclusively forecast they would. In fact, as a man well known for wrong predictions this one was pretty spectacular in its inaccuracy – *NIL POINTS* – as the bird in the Eurovision Song Contest used to say!

Left: Marco Van Basten – England's executioner

Below: Another Dutch master, Rijkaard, robs Lineker and Beardsley

But while our performance was disappointing to say the least, don't expect me to join the media bandwagon and call for the head of Bobby Robson. Let's face it the man guided England to the last eight in the World Cup and the last eight in the European Championship ... and that's just about where we stand in the world rankings at the moment – in the top ten football nations.

As an Englishman of course it hurt to see us lose unluckily to the Republic, compete and lose to the multi-talented Dutch and get ripped apart by the Russians.

But don't tell me any manager around would do better than Robbo – I don't believe it, and no-one in the game, including Brian Clough, believes it either. The truth of the matter is we don't have too many great players in our midst at the moment ... Bryan Robson and Gary Lineker are our only world-class competitors now that Peter Shilton has passed his prime.

So when I read headlines like 'On Yer Bike Robbo', 'Robson Must Go', etc., I think to myself, 'What the hell do you lot know?' Some of the press witch-hunting which went on after the Championships was a disgrace and most of it was from people who have never played the game at any level whatsoever.

The truth of the matter is that the defensive weaknesses Saint and I had been highlighting for almost two years – the weakness through the middle – finally became fully exposed in the full glare of the Championships.

And I've got news for any aspiring England manager ... you ain't gonna do any better mate ... even if Terry Butcher is available to play.

For to my mind Bobby Robson, Brian Clough, Howard Kendall, Terry Venables, Graham Taylor, or any other prospective

Bobby Robson – slated, but who would be better?

England manager, hasn't a prayer of competing at the highest level with the likes of West Germany, Italy, Holland or the USSR unless there is a wholesale change to the sweeper system not only at international level but throughout the English League.

I'm not knocking our football ... it's exciting, it's robust and it's entertaining. But it is founded on the offside rule ... and we are probably the only nation in Europe that caters for it.

We base our game on the ability of a referee and two linesmen to spot players stepping over the defensive line. If the flag doesn't go up then the team defending is in trouble. It's no coincidence that throughout Europe the sweeper system is a well-oiled operation.

In Italy they don't talk about offside traps – they are alien to the game in Spaghetti land – the sweeper system sees to that.

I'll tell you what, I would have loved to play against our present system. Give me a one-to-one situation with any goalkeeper and I'd fancy my chances ... I might not score every time but I reckon I'd score nine times out of ten.

Let's face it, referees and linesmen are fallible ... and so is our present system. In my humble opinion Robbo should introduce a sweeper system into the England set-up... then we might be able to compete with the great nations. The Viallis, Van Bastens and Vollers of the world might think twice about bursting through to be met by someone like Bryan Robson mopping up at the back of our defence.

Which brings me nicely to my thoughts on Bryan being given the sweeper's role. Bobby Robson has disagreed publicly with me on my feeling that the United skipper should be pulled back in to the libero position. He says:

'Trouble is Jim – Bryan is also my best midfield player.' I give him that, but my attitude is that we have more midfielders around than hard, decisive, quick players who could give that vital cover at the back. Robson could fill a present-day Bobby Moore role for England, I'm convinced of that.

Anyway it's time players such as Paul Gascoigne, Steve McMahon, John Barnes and maybe even Peter Beardsley were given their chance in midfield.

For a start Peter Beardsley, despite his huge talent, does not convince me that he is a true quality striker. He is a clever little player who will not score a lot of goals at international level. He scored a beauty against Scotland last May and that was that. In fact it's interesting that England's only two goals in the European Championship were scored by defenders ... Bryan Robson and Tony Adams.

Gary Lineker – not a good championship, but still world class

Having mentioned that, I exonerate Gary Lineker of all blame in West Germany. He had an off day against the Irish, where he should have scored four goals and didn't. And he will rightly blame himself for the early chance which struck a post against Holland ... that has got to go down as a bad miss.

But Lineker is an exciting player. As a former striker I know it's impossible to hit the target all of the time. Gary, though, would never be out of any team I picked ... he'll score in any company.

So my advice to Bobby Robson is ... get the defence right and take it from there. You aren't too far away you know and if it's any consolation old mate, Alf Ramsey, contrary to many people's opinion, didn't get it right either until when it mattered during the World Cup finals in 1966.

It's amazing how time clouds reality. I speak to people who criticise Bobby Robson and then say 'It wasn't like that in your day Greavsie ... old Sir Alf had it well organised hadn't he?' The answer is an emphatic 'NO!'

In fact, Alf hadn't a clue what his best side was going into the 1966 World Cup finals ... he tried three different wingers in our opening match – Alan Ball, Terry Paine and Ian Callaghan. That didn't work. And it's worth remembering that Martin Peters played only one game before the final and that Geoff Hurst wasn't considered a regular either.

I was an anomaly in Alf's system because I was a bit of a maverick, and, while the World Cup Final team is indelibly etched in football and folks' minds now, only the likes of Gordon Banks, Bobby Moore, Ray Wilson, Bobby Charlton and myself were considered regulars.

The point I'm making is that Bobby Robson probably had a more settled side than Alf did. Luckily it happened for Ramsey ... it didn't in West Germany for Bobby Robson. But if the FA stick by their guns and let him carry on until Italy in 1990 it just might.

Anyway I've a question to ask the press who were screaming for Robson's head after West Germany: who would they give the job to?

Let's look at the contenders. There is, of course, Brian Clough ... but I reckon it's too late now for Cloughie. He should have been given the job before Ron Greenwood after the Don Revie shambles.

But can any of the pressmen who are calling for Clough really see Brian turning up at the FA Headquarters in that old green sweatshirt with his squash racquet under his arm?

Let's face it, Cloughie has been a law unto himself over the years. I'm his biggest admirer, but he is used to getting his own way at Forest. His chairman and directors don't feel comfortable unless he's slagged them off at least once a month and I have the feeling that the old boy is a bit past travelling to foreign shores to spy on any likely opposition.

It should be noted too that, when Robson was being crucified in West Germany, Brian was right on the phone to let him know he wasn't after his job ... no matter what the press were inventing. He meant it too.

Howard Kendall, Terry Venables and Graham Taylor are all being tipped as likely successors, but are they likely to do better than Bobby Robson after his six years' experience? Very unlikely I think.

The trouble is some of the pressmen who tried to act as executioners are so far up certain managers' backsides they can see their tonsils move. They want their man to have the job so badly they turn their newspapers into a propaganda sheet. I'm surprised their editors allow it ... it's only one man's opinion of the situation ... and it is so cruel I cannot believe it.

For the uninitiated Bobby Robson doesn't just pick England teams. His is a 24-hour-a-day job, where he acts as an ambassador for his country. I know Robbo. He is a conscientious man.

It would be easy for him to send someone else to spy on the opposition, to turn up at schools' and amateur football clubs' nights out, to meet sponsors putting money into the game, to greet foreign dignitaries. He will not do so because he knows that these tasks are part of the job of being England manager. To my mind he has been a first-class manager and a fine ambassador for the game in this country.

I'm loath to admit it, but perhaps the Scots have got it right. They didn't qualify for the European Championship finals, but there was no cry for Andy Roxburgh's head. The Scots are more passionate than we English about their football team, but they realise that at present they have no great players around and that until their national team inherits, as it will, fresh exciting talent they have no divine right to success.

Roxburgh is experimenting with youth north of the border ... so should Bobby Robson. Certain players let him down in West Germany and they should be replaced. Personally I'd like to see the likes of John Fashanu, Paul Gascoigne and young Nigel Clough given their chance. Too many of our present squad have been promising youngsters for too long.

I had fifty-seven caps for England ... the first when I was nineteen, the last when I

Bobby Robson putting heart and soul into England

21

was twenty-seven. If you're good enough you're old enough.

Like Saint I feel that one of the vital ingredients missing in today's international scene is fun ... I think back to my days in an England shirt and remember not only the goals and the victories but also the laughs ... I don't see too many smiles these days. It's all too heavy, too pressurised.

Let's face it, I didn't have too much to smile about in my debut ... it was in a South American tour match against Peru ... we lost 4-1! Mind you I did have the consolation of scoring the goal. But there was no talk of a crisis!

It's strange how fate plays the cards. That tour was also the great Billy Wright's last England tour. I played alongside Billy when we beat America 8-1. Later I was to team up with the old boy again. Me as an inexperienced newcomer to television ... Billy as head of sport at Central Television. He was a great player and has been a great boss.

Like I've said, the England squads were fun in those far-off days ... especially on trips abroad.

I remember Rio in 1964 ... and so does Bobby Moore ... for that was the occasion Pele turned on all the old Brazilian magic and had Moore twisting and turning so much he seemed to be screwed into the ground like a corkscrew.

We were beaten 5-1 at the Maracana and were lucky it was only five. Yet in those days there was no cry for our manager's head. The press reports were only of the wonderful talent of the Brazilians and how we might learn from their skills.

Well one thing we players did learn...

'Fat Boy' Gascoigne – one who deserves a chance

Copacabana kids – taught us a thing or two!

never take on the kids of the Copacabana Beach.

After the match a few of us hit the pubs of Rio ... I remember Bobby Moore, George Eastham, Johnny 'Budgie' Byrne, John Connolly and Gordon Banks plus yours truly having a right few beers.

Dawn rises early on the Copacabana and as usual the street urchins gathered for their twenty-four-hour-long football matches. It was decided that we would take them on ... and we did, only to lose by an even bigger score than we had the night before at the Maracana!

Anyone wondering just how the Brazilians year after year keep discovering such wonderful talent need only take a trip to the Copacabana Beach ... it certainly opened our bloodshot eyes. Those kids were sheer magic. They took us apart with a bewildering display of ball skills ... and I noticed one thing – they never let a ball hit the ground. Because the sand would deaden it, they controlled the ball with body, thigh or toe before it hit the ground ... and that's

something I've noticed Brazilian international sides do at all times. The skills of Copacabana last them a lifetime.

That beach lesson from those dusky kids left Budgie Byrne a bit hot and bothered. He opted for a dip in the surf ... and almost drowned. The current was strong and we had to drag him back to shore spluttering like a stranded cod.

Of course, he got little sympathy only some heavy mickey-taking. But as usual Johnny got his own back. That night as we prepared to go to an Embassy reception in Rio, togged up in England blazer and flannels, Budgie gave me a gentle nudge and I wound up in the hotel pool.

It's strange, I hadn't been happy with my blazer ... it had been too big from the start ... but it cleaned up lovely and had shrunk just enough to be a perfect fit. It's an ill wave! All innocent fun of course – shared by the press corps of the day. But, unlike today, there were no banner headlines of high jinks in the England camp, etc. How times have changed.

George Eastham was a big mate of mine in England days and as a bit of a punter he was always on the lookout for any inside information – horses or dogs.

As it happened in those days I used to run a greyhound called Burren Bridge and before one game George came to me and said: 'I see your mutt is running at Brighton – any chance?'

Fancying myself as a bit of an expert I told him 'No chance. It's an open race over 660 yards and it's out of its class. Don't touch it with a barge pole.'

But George didn't listen. Instead he took a collection of a few quid from each England player and took himself off to plunge it on Burren Bridge with the local bookie – we were staying at Hendon Hall at the time.

The next morning George came up to me

and slapped me on the back. 'Well done Greavsie... what a winner... 25-1. The lads have had a nice little touch.'

I thought it was some kind of wind-up... but it wasn't. The bloody dog had romped in at 25-1 and the local bookie was skint. The only bloke who didn't win a penny was myself. After that I decided greyhound racing was not for J.G.

It should be noted that George and I, during the 1966 World Cup campaign, finished as the all sports champions of England. To pass time at Hendon Hall during the World Cup we played every sport from snooker to squash, from tennis to badminton.

George and I were teamed together and lifted the trophy as all-round champions... a month later we both missed out on a World Cup Winners medal!

Alan Ball was only a youngster in that World Cup squad, but Bally was some player – a non-stop dynamo who had the cheek of the devil. It was hard to pull one over on the little man... he was always on the alert for a wind-up, but there was one occasion when he had all of us plus 200 chairs falling about.

The incident happened after my last game for England... a 1-0 win over Austria in Vienna. Bally had scored the goal, and following the banquet we all hit the town to celebrate. A group of us finished up in the bar of the ballroom of our hotel and late on in walked a flushed Ball.

'We won. We won,' he shouted and stumbled backwards... knocking over row upon row of folding chairs. The domino effect was amazing and the racket unbelievable... Bally's face was the same colour as his hair as we all roared with laughter. Again the press were present... but the incident remained private.

What would today's pressmen have made of the man who used to nick out of England's hotel on matchdays to do the shopping for his wife? It happened during our day... and the offender was my old Spurs and England striking partner Bobby Smith.

I roomed with Bobby at Hendon Hall and I used to be puzzled at him taking off on a Saturday morning before an important international and disappearing until lunchtime. He would never tell me where he had gone, but my missus Irene came up with the answer. She told me, 'I know what he does... he goes home and does the shopping for Mavis.'

I couldn't believe it, but it was true, Smithy lived in Palmers Green, only four or five miles from Hendon, and he wasn't going to

break his Saturday morning routine for anything. He would skip out to the local supermarket and fill the trolley for his missus before slipping back into our hotel. To be fair though he never actually shopped in his England strip!

One of the biggest laughs I had at semi-top level came after I had quit playing for England. Bobby Moore and Sir Stanley Matthews were asked to pick a team on behalf of BP to take on a Kuwaiti International Squad in Kuwait ... and I was chosen to make the trip.

Now Sir Stan at the time must have been around fifty-five and of course still a tremendous athlete. But the temperature in that stadium was around 120 degrees and as the game went on we noticed that the great man was melting on the wing.

Mooro gave the nod to big Dave Underwood, a great London character who was acting as manager, to get Sir Stan off ... but Matthews being a shrewdie and full of pride clocked the move and drifted to the far wing.

Underwood was up against it, but he came through like a trooper. He jumped into the stand and through the loudspeaker boomed 'Let's have a big hand for the one and only Sir Stanley Matthews, who is now coming off.'

The crowd gave Stan a standing ovation, and smiling through clenched teeth he duly departed the scene!

For the record, we won 4-3 - a team of has-beens against the Kuwaiti National XI of the time. Not a bad result, and yours truly scored the winner ... a header from, would you believe, an accurate cross from Jimmy Hill. Now there's an unusual double for you!

I'm often asked who were the most talented people I played with or against. Well, I'm on record as saying that George Best was the greatest talent I ever came up against and that I rate Pele as the best ever all round player, but there were a few players in my day who to my mind were unsung heroes.

Johnny Haynes of Fulham and England was a man with an extraordinary amount of talent. Haynesie, of course, was England's first £100 footballer and he did a marvellous job for Fulham, but I think he should have moved to a bigger club.

He did in fact get the chance to move to Tottenham when John White was killed by lightning, but declined the move. I think he made a mistake there ... his talent deserved a bigger stage than Craven Cottage. For Johnny had wonderful vision. He could pass the ball through the eye of a needle and to my mind was an England great.

Another man who did not get the credit his skills deserved was that marvellous little right winger from Blackburn Rovers, Bryan Douglas.

Bryan was a fifty fags a day man ... he used to have a permanent brown scorch mark on his lips ... but he could play. He could torment the greatest full backs in the game, but sadly – possibly because he came in the wake of the great Matthews – he never got the praise he should have. He was most under-rated.

It's strange, by the way, to think now about how many of our England team smoked in those days. I did and so did the Charlton boys Jack and Bobby ... and although he didn't admit it so did the great Sir Alf.

Actually Alf never let on to being a smoker, but he used to nip off to the loo to have a sly puff ... what he didn't know was that the entire England team used to spy on him for a laugh.

The great man would take himself off, find himself a cubicle and sit himself down. A few seconds later up would come a puff of white smoke and we players waiting outside would have a chortle: the R.C.s in the squad would joke 'it's Pope Alfred the First.'

It was hard not to titter when at training later Alf used to lecture us on the effects of smoking! Mind you Alf was due his secret puff ... he won us the World Cup and that's not too likely to happen again for a while.

As I've said things have changed since those old days with England. We used to get

Jackie Charlton – the only 'Irishman' with a Geordie accent!

£30 a man plus third-class rail fares as expenses . . . and to a man we were panicking when putting in our expenses.

We always tried to diddle a few extra bob, but the FA Treasurer used to question us about the exact fare from home to London. Many a time I was in a blind sweat over diddling half a crown!

We did of course all benefit from the World Cup win. Every squad member was given a £1000 bonus ... and then we got an immediate demand from the tax man! The demand – quite ridiculous when you think of it – was taken to court and the players won. We got our £1000 intact and for once the Inland Revenue went away empty-handed.

Despite that lawsuit, though, money was not as important to players then as it appears to be today. I understand that football and sponsorship must live hand in hand in today's commercial world ... but I do believe it has all gone over the top.

There's little fun left in sport any more ... everything is so immaculate ... so precise. Excellence has become boring. People like Ivan Lendl, Martina Navratilova, Steve Davis are all expert in their craft, but it is somehow too immaculate. There are no smiles. No lasting friendships.

I watched Maurice Setters sitting with Jack Charlton in the Republic's dug-out during the European Championships and remembered how he used to kick me black and blue as Manchester United's captain. But I know, like Tommy Smith, if we met tomorrow he would hug me like a long lost friend because of those battles long ago.

Will the present-day footballers behave in the same way thirty years from now ... I doubt it.

When I visit football grounds these days I find them eerie places.

Following the European Championships Jack Charlton commented that if, as manager of the Republic, he was ever subjected to the same type of press abuse as Bobby Robson he would quit football. Jack, like many others, cares about the game, but he realises I'm sure that the atmosphere has changed ... and not for the better.

The Irish are on a high and being Irish they might just stay there ... after all not many countries have been given a massive spontaneous public reception upon returning from a tournament without qualifying.

But that's perhaps the difference between the English and the Irish. We demand success. The Irish are happy with brave failure. Our demands are wrong and we must change if football, as big Jack and I knew it, is to return to normality.

Nowadays I'm inclined to think of the contorted faces of fans as they spit out songs of hatred at the visiting support rather than the spectacle of the game itself.

Yet these are the self same stadiums where in better days laughing happy people came to enjoy the skills and drama of the game ... many of them with kids perched on their shoulders. The only songs these people knew were team songs and visitors were welcomed, not reviled.

It's sad to think that that has all gone and may never return. Sportswriter Laurie Pignon once wrote in the *Daily Mail*: 'I regret to say what has finally left the game is fun.'

I have to agree with that. Luckily though some of us still have our memories to cheer us up.

3 SAINT CHARACTERS

Perhaps I am getting older, but I'm beginning to agree with the people who say there are not the same amount of characters in the game as there were in the playing days of Greavsie and myself.

Sure, there are still great players around ... Bryan Robson, Glenn Hoddle, John Barnes, Ian Rush, Paul McStay, Norman Whiteside and many others would have made it in the teams of our day – make no mistake about that. There is no substitute for skill.

But the fun stories from the dressing-rooms seem to be getting fewer and fewer. Maybe it's because the game has become so professional and commercial. Nowadays the salaries are so big that any player would be gambling for high stakes if he was to do anything that upset the boss and cost him his first-team place.

But I can't help feeling that the free-wheeling days of the sixties and seventies did have a bit more sparkle to them ... a bit more fun ... and certainly the characters will live in my memory for ever.

Later in the book I offer readers a 'Dish of Scouse' ... a pot-pourri of Liverpool-based stories from past and present which help make my adopted home town a fun place to be.

And when I think of characters in the game I can't help thinking about great players such as former Everton heroes Gordon West, Alex Young, Sandy Brown and Alan Ball - all great players, but who would do anything for a laugh.

Gordon West, as any older Merseyside fan will tell you, was my prime target whenever I took the field in a Liverpool derby match.

The big fellow was a marvellous goal-keeper both for the Blues and England, but there was no love lost when we were in opposition.

In fact it got to the stage that our confrontations became part of the folklore of Everton–Liverpool derbies, such was the apparent intensity of the hatred between us.

If the truth be told we both played to the crowd. It was always guns drawn at high noon ... and the fans lapped it up.

Westie and I had many a battle and we were always desperately trying to pull one over on the other, and towards the end of my career at Anfield the big fellow almost delivered the *coup de grâce*.

It was a grotty spring day as I remember, all mud and guts, and the ball was flying from end to end when we won a corner on the right. As the ball came over I made the usual beeline for Westie and made to swing a punch at him. It was the usual confrontation, but I pulled the punch ... but Westie went down as if he were poleaxed.

As the referee marched towards me I shouted 'Get up Westie – you'll get me sent off.' Around us all hell was breaking loose, but as I looked down I could see a little grin on Gordon's face ... I was going to get my come-uppance in no uncertain manner ... an early bath.

As I said Greavsie – Gordon West was good!

It was then the linesman came to my rescue. As the ref was about to send me off the stand linesman called him over ... he had seen the incident and Westie's wind-up was scuppered.

Suddenly he was up on his feet with a grin as large as the Mersey tunnel. 'Nearly Saint,' he shouted, wagging his finger. In the end we had the last laugh though ... we won the game.

Gordon in fact did have the final painful say in our clashes ... that came in my very last Liverpool–Everton derby match. Shanks was a cunning old fox and I've often wondered if he was looking for me to have a bad match just to send me on my way with the approval of the fans. Certainly he stitched me up lovely with his tactics in my last derby.

Alan Ball was at the height of his fame. A red-headed ball of fire whose young legs took him all over the park ... you can be sure that no-one in our team wanted the job of marking Bally. Yet Shanks gave the job to me!

As I say, I was nearing the end of my career at Anfield and that game sealed it. I was totally out of place as a marker and Alan ran me ragged. I tell you I visited parts of Anfield that day I'd never seen before.

It finally dawned on me that this was going to be my last derby match, so I thought: 'I've got to get Westie somehow.' Near the end we won a corner and I gave up the hopeless task of containing Ball to join in the fray. As the ball came over I hurtled in to the mass of red and blue jerseys – looking to upset my great adversary possibly for the last time.

I didn't hit the ball but I did hit something ... for I finished up in hospital nursing a broken hand. Needless to say big Gordon's mischievous handshake at the end of the game was not accepted.

People often ask if our own Liverpool team was better than today's. It's difficult to judge ... after all you can only be the best in your own era. But one thing I do know, the opposition was tougher in those days.

Apart from ourselves Spurs had a wonderful side which included, of course, the one and only Greavsie. Now Jimmy doesn't know this, but he was one of only two people Shankly would afford the compliment of man-marking in any game.

He used to tell our defence: 'Watch that Greavsie ... he's a poacher ... he's always almost off-side and one of these times the linesman will get fed up flagging and let him get away with it. If you don't hold him you're dead.'

And he was right too. Jimmy used to haunt

Gordon Banks – one of the greats

'The Menace' – on and off the park!

the offside trap, and at least once a game, with defenders holding their hands up in appeal, quick as a flash he'd find the net.

The other man we used to adopt a man-marking policy for was the great George Best, who, of course, was part of that marvellous Manchester United team of the sixties made up of stars such as Charlton, Law, Crerand, Stiles, etc.

Now George to my mind was the most skilful player I ever played against... and I know Greavsie shares my views. A will-o'-the-wisp, he was an amazing player. He could run, shoot, pass balls short, long and even tackle... yet he looked all of four stone soaking wet!

He was another player no-one in our team wanted the job of marking. The man could turn you like a corkscrew and frequently did. Now Tommy Smith was fearless and a first-

class player, but I've often seen him shake his head in amazement as George would dance his way past him before slinging in one of those deadly accurate crosses of his. Believe me those Smith–Best confrontations were worth the entrance money alone to Liverpool–United matches.

Make no mistake United were a great side ... and they had marvellous characters too ... like my old Scottish team-mates Pat Crerand and Denis Law.

Pat was one of the best passers of a football ever. Never the quickest ... I well remember Shanks saying: 'Now Crerand – watch him – he's slower than you think' – but he could split a defence in the twinkling of an eye with those great crossfield passes. He was also a good mate and good companion.

Denis too was a marvel. Quicksilver in the box you just couldn't pin him down... and

The one and only Bestie . . . sheer genius

that was off the park too. I remember one visit we had to Manchester United. Denis went off injured, and after the game Paddy, who had offered to put my wife Betsy and I up for the night at his home, said: 'Let's go find Law.'

Off we went into deepest Manchester and we eventually arrived at a working men's snooker club. There was Denis coolly potting a few reds. To my amazement he looked up and grinned: 'Hello lads ... how did it finish?' He hadn't even waited to the end of the game! The final score Denis, if you read this, was 1-1.

Another great character in those days was the England goalkeeper Gordon Banks, who to my mind was one of the greatest ever.

He certainly gave me some heartache... particularly in the FA Cup semi-final tie with Leicester at Hillsborough in 1963. We were favourites to win but lost 1-0 after Banksie had put on a wonderful show of goalkeeping. We hit him with everything but the kitchen-sink but he stood firm and Leicester and not Liverpool went through to face Spurs in the Final.

Mind you, to this day, Banksie still winds me up about the hate mail he got from Anfield fans following that match ... all down to a newspaper photograph.

The picture taken at the end of the game showed me coming off heart-broken and Gordon, right behind me, apparently laughing at my misery. He was not laughing at me of course ... he was just happy at having made the Final ... But the Liverpool press made a big thing of it all ... and the hate mail started to pour in on poor Banksie.

In the end though the Kop, who have always show a deep affection for great goalkeeping, took Gordon to their hearts. After the pain of missing that Cup Final had passed, he was to be given a standing ovation every time he kept goal at Anfield. He deserved it, too.

In the same era of course was the immaculate Bobby Moore ... captain of England and West Ham United ... and one of the biggest characters in the game ... then and now.

Now Bobby, as Greavsie often tells, is one of the great lager drinkers of all time. While the rest of us would be having a nip of whisky, Bacardi and Coke, vodka and orange, Mooro would stay on the pints and drink us all under the table.

'He must have the bladder of a bull,' says the bold Jim ... and certainly, as someone who has enjoyed Bobby's company on the occasional night out, I wouldn't dispute that!

Bobby of course was a wonderful player. His anticipation was magnificent. Bill Shankly used to say: 'The first two yards are in your head,' and Mooro proved that. He could read a game perfectly, and while I don't agree entirely with Greavsie's gag that Bobby couldn't tackle, run or head a ball, there's no doubt in my mind that he was the greatest ever at closing down the opposition play ... reading exactly where the ball was going to be. He didn't have the first two yards in his head, he had four.

Bobby of course was part of the great West Ham United squad of the sixties who all loved a night out and a few beers. I hasten to add that they could play a bit as well ... you don't have a bad team with the likes of Bobby Moore, Clyde Best, Brian Dear, Martin Peters, Geoff Hurst and big John Cushley in your line-up.

All great lads ... but don't mention that to the wife. For on one hilarious occasion she fell foul of the best drinkers in football ... and it didn't do Jimmy Tarbuck's Rolls-Royce too much good!

Betsy and I had arranged a weekend in London with Tarby and his wife Pauline, and Jimmy, the toast of the town, was due to meet us at Euston with his pride and joy ... no, not his wife ... his new white Rolls-Royce, which he had just bought from Tom Jones.

All was well until we realised that we were on the same train as Mooro and the West Ham lads. Bobby, as usual the perfect gentleman, invited us back to their compartment and soon the drinks and the stories began to flow.

Now as I've said Mooro was dangerous. Very few men could drink one for one with Bobby and live to remember the tale. So Betsy had no chance, although she tried valiantly to keep up with the boys. By the time we arrived at Euston and waved an unsteady goodbye to Bobby and the chaps, Betsy was well and truly gone. And yours truly wasn't too clever either.

Tarbuck found it all very amusing ... until Betsy *en route* to the restaurant suddenly felt rather ill. A frantic scramble to open the Rolls window failed ... they were electrically operated ... and the white Rolls-Royce suddenly wasn't immaculate any more.

Tarby has never let the missus live the incident down and the message is clear for anyone who doesn't know ... don't try and keep up with Bobby Moore and his lagers!

One great character I had the honour of playing against and later knowing was the fantastic Johan Cruyff of Ajax and Holland. Who will ever forget those wonderful World Cup competitions in West Germany and Argentina when Holland twice made the

The great Cruyff – his magic brought *glasnost* before Gorbachev

final only to fail twice ... unluckily to my mind on both occasions.

My first encounter with Cruyff came in the fog of Amsterdam in one of our early European ties. We had drawn 2-2 at Anfield with a sparkling young Ajax side, and despite Shanks's usual optimism we knew we were in for a tough time away.

And so it proved. Cruyff and company took us apart 5-1 on a foggy night with a spellbinding display of the same total football Holland were to go on to show internationally.

While Shanks grumbled: 'How can anyone expect us to win against a side that don't want to play football,' we all realised that we had come across a superstar of football in the making.

One amusing incident from that match sticks in my mind. Bobby Graham, a smashing little inside forward whom I later took to Motherwell as a player, was one of Shankly's scapegoats in that match. Looking for any excuse, he raved at Bobby: 'And you Graham ... you were hiding in the fog out there.'

Later, after Cruyff had joined Barcelona, I got an amazing insight into how football can break the most stubborn of barriers. Anglia commentator Gerry Harrison and myself were given the unenviable job of prising something from the Soviet camp ... but all we got all afternoon for our troubles was a dour 'Niet!'

Then Johan Cruyff, who lived in a house on the hill above the training complex, arrived. He recognised us and began talking about the World Cup and his time at Barcelona. Suddenly the Russians noticed the great man and *glasnost* happened.

36

Puskas – the galloping major lines up for Hungary at Wembley in 1953. The Magyars won 6–3!

European Footballer of the Year, presented Johan with a beautiful *balalaika* as a token of their esteem.

Cruyff was genuinely touched, and so were we. The Soviets had recognised Cruyff for what he was, a superstar of soccer, and for half an hour the Cold War was forgotten.

It was another World Cup campaign – in England in 1966 – that gave me one of my most memorable moments ever. I had gone to Manchester to watch Hungary play Bulgaria, and I was jostling through the crowds with a friend when a well-known face came pushing towards us. Besieged by autograph hunters, it was the great Ferenc Puskas, the magical Magyar whose skills destroyed England at Wembley in the fifties and who sparked that wonderful Real Madrid team of the sixties.

Puskas had always been one of my great heroes, and as we stood back and watched the great man he came right over to me, said hello and shook my hand. I was dumbstruck. Puskas had recognised me.

It's worth remembering that I was at that time Scotland's regular centre forward and had scored the winning goal in Liverpool's first ever Cup Final victory ... but there was I acting like a star-struck kid in front of one of my great heroes. I'll never forget that moment.

Talking about that Cup Final goal in 1965 I'm often asked if I remember much about it ... the answer is very definitely 'Yes'.

The game is indelibly etched in my mind. We were at 1–1 in extra time with Leeds United through goals by Roger Hunt and Billy Bremner when Ian Callaghan crossed from the right. It was an awkward angle but I somehow got my head to the ball, and I knew as soon as it left my forehead it was in. I can still see the spray coming off the net as the ball hit it. Gary Sprake in the Leeds goal

They were so excited at meeting him ... he was invited into their little compound and they gathered around him like excited schoolkids looking for autographs, taking pictures and talking excitedly to him about their chances and the World Cup in general.

The final accolade came when Oleg Blokhin, their star player, who was once

My memory of a lifetime – the goal which brought the FA Cup to Anfield

had no chance and I had a memory to last the rest of my life.

Being a Scot of course many of my memories are of great Scottish characters... people like Mackay, McNeill, Hamilton, Law, Crerand and Jim Baxter.

Many of these characters appeared in our first book, but one Baxter story still makes me laugh. Jim of course was a wonderful player. A classy wing-half with a left foot gifted from God and cheeky with it. Slim Jim was world class ... and he knew it.

It was one disastrous close-season tour with Scotland. Don't forget that our Scotland team in the sixties was one of the best ever... in fact although I say it myself I've yet to see one so accomplished... so when we headed out for a tour of Norway and Eire we were expected to eat up the opposition.

Perhaps we were a bit too complacent... certainly Jim got off on the wrong foot. He arrived with us at Glasgow Airport with a large carrier bag, and in it was £1500 in readies, a lot of money in those days.

It transpired that he had been on the razzle all night and had ended up taking a casino for £1500. Not having time to bank it before we left he had to take it with him... and Billy McNeill was given the job of watching it (Jim couldn't have trusted the rest of us!).

Obviously with that kind of loot there would be fun and games on the tour, and so it proved.

We were beaten 4–3 by Norway – who at that time were looked upon as Scandinavian no-hopers – and after the game we adjourned to a Bergen beer bar.

It all started innocently enough – someone accidentally spilled beer over someone else and before we knew it the whole thing had developed into a beer-throwing contest.

Naturally we were not Bergen's favourite sons, and when we finally made it back to the team's hotel the selectors headed by SFA Secretary Willie Allan were still sitting up – and looking none too pleased. All was well though until Baxter arrived and caught

sight of that great Rangers player Jimmy Millar, who had given Jim a soaking at the beer palace.

Before the entire SFA hierarchy, the bold Jim grabbed a jug of water and threw it over Millar. That was too much for Willie Allan to take. A feisty little character, he demanded 'Baxter – behave.'

By this time the place was in uproar and we players knew that Baxter, being Baxter, wouldn't take that. Again Allan roared: 'Baxter – sit down.'

Jim, cheeky as ever, replied: 'It's Mr Baxter to you ... and, by the way, stick your team ... I'm off home tomorrow.'

Now Baxter was a superstar. If he lived up to his promise and walked out the next day it would be front page headlines and the SFA knew it. Our manager Ian McColl, who was later to take Jim to Sunderland, was given the job of talking Slim Jim out of his threat. He managed it but it didn't do us much good ... we lost 1–0 to the Republic and were in the doghouse again.

People often ask me how good was Baxter. The answer is 'magical'.

He not only had wonderful ability he also had an air of confidence about him which permeated through a team. And with the likes of Mackay, Law and Alex Hamilton around him he had pretty good back-up.

When I look back over the years Hamilton or 'Hammy' surely was one of the biggest characters in football never snapped up by a top English side. Alex was a Dundee man but he had all the swagger of a superstar ... and he was a marvellous little full back, speedy, quick in the tackle, and ever ready to race upfield to aid his forwards.

Now, as I've said, that Scotland team

'Slim' Jim Baxter – so gifted and with the cheek of the devil on and off the pitch was useful. The regular line-up was Brown (Spurs), Hamilton (Dundee), Caldow (Rangers), Crerand/Mackay, McNeill, Baxter, Scott/Henderson, White, St John, Law and Wilson ... not a bad outfit and fairly unstoppable when on song.

Hammy always reminded me of a chipmunk with his toothy grin and bristle-topped haircut ... and he had the cheek of one too. He was no respecter of reputations, and when it came to his turn in team talks Ian McColl would say: 'Now Hammy you've got to take care of Bobby Charlton.' Hammy would pat his hip pocket and say: 'No bother boss ... I've got him in my hippy.'

And you knew he regularly had too!

Hammy got away with murder, for the English lads liked his company... but on one occasion he strained their patience a bit. It was in 1962 and we had just beaten England 2–0 at Hampden. It was Scotland's first victory over the Auld Enemy since the war and we were in high spirits... especially Hammy.

At the after-match banquet the party was in full flow when Hammy came up with a real showstopper by shouting: 'Hey trainer get back downstairs and open up that hamper... I've forgotten to take Charlton out of my back pocket!' Messrs Charlton and Co. were not amused.

Alex loved a singsong, and his special party trick was to get on the piano. He was a fair piano player, and a few years later in South Africa he had me in stitches with one escapade.

It was at the end of my career... and of his. We were both playing for South African teams and we met up in Port Elizabeth... nothing would do but we must have a party ... and Hammy was the supreme fixer.

We were set to have a rare old time until Hammy noticed he didn't have one necessary ingredient ... a piano ... so off he went in search of one. Ten minutes later there was a great commotion out in the street ... someone was tinkling the ivories ... and that had to be our Alex.

But to our amazement he was perched on the back of a truck playing the piano. He had picked up the instrument at a friend's house, hoisted it onto the truck, and was giving everyone in Port Elizabeth a touch of the Winifred Atwells as he travelled through the city.

Needless to say the party was a belter.

I suppose I learned pretty early that football was a game of characters. I was a teenager at Motherwell when I learned that players can go a little astray.

In those days we had a full back called Rab McCallum, who like many before and after was smitten by the gambling bug.

Now Rab was a family man and in those days in the fifties the game was not awash with cash as it is today... particularly not at Fir Park. So every pay day Rab's wife used to wait for him outside the front door to ensure she got her cash before the bookie.

But Rab was cute. After training he would leg it over the back wall and through the little school adjoining Fir Park, leaving his missus tearing her hair out.

Eventually she got just as cute as Rab and was waiting at the entrance of the school. Rab was done like a kipper ... and his gambling days were over.

Those were great days at Fir Park and some of my team-mates from those far-off times are still amongst my best friends today. People such as Pat Quinn, Willie Hunter, Bobby Roberts and the like ... all fine players who moved on to greater things with other clubs and Scotland. And whenever we get together we talk about my going away do!

Bob Paisley – his dug-out antics landed him in trouble

I was *en route* to Liverpool and decided to have a night out for the lads. For some unknown reason it was decided that Edinburgh should be the venue, despite the fact that we all lived in the West of Scotland.

Pat Quinn was the driver and we took along a friend ... Willie White the brother of Davie, who was to become manager of Rangers. Poor Willie he didn't know what he was letting himself in for.

When we reached Edinburgh Bobby Roberts mentioned that Davie Gibson, who at that time played for Hibs (and who went on to star for Leicester and Scotland), would like to join in... there was one problem, he was playing for the army at Berwick that night.

No problem ... we all then motored down to Berwick to pick up Davie. The night out had the look of disaster, and so it proved.

We duly watched Davie star for the army and then got totally legless in Berwick... with the result that while Pat Quinn and I somehow got a train back to Glasgow and

Motherwell poor Willie White was stranded in Berwick ... and had to stay the night at the KOSB barracks there.

I stumbled back into my house as dawn broke to be fronted by Mrs White. 'Where's my husband?' she demanded.

'Berwick,' I replied.

'What, North Berwick?' she asked incredulously.

'No, Berwick-on-Tweed.'

'But that's in England... you don't go to England for a night out,' she shrieked.

'We did,' said I, and then flopped out on the floor.

At that time I hadn't a clue that Willie was in the able hands of the Kosbies. The next day Willie and Hunter turned up at my house ... Willie facing hell from his missus and Hunter minus his watch and holes all over his trousers. 'We'll be glad to see the back of you,' they chorused. Fine friends, them!

Once in England of course I was in the hands of civilised people... or so I thought... then came the fun with Shankly and of course Bob Paisley.

Now Bob is usually a quiet man, but on one occasion he got himself locked up for going over the top with his touchline antics.

It happened during a friendly match in Majorca, fixed to give players a few bob for the holiday trip. The referee, a dogmatic Spaniard, kept at Bob and Reuben Bennett in our dug-out as they shouted instructions ... Shanks was on holiday.

Old Bob ignored the ref, and after a few more roars from the touchline the ref called in the Guardia and Bob was frogmarched to the dressing-room, where he was locked up by the police for the remainder of the match!

During my days as manager of Motherwell I had as my coach at Fir Park a real character in the shape of little Billy Hodgson,

who was a fine little winger with Leicester City and Sheffield Utd.

Now Billy's love of football, like many coaches, has taken him to some strange places: Africa, the Far East, Scandinavia... and Iceland.

I used to tell him he was in the running for the gypsy of the year award – he seemed to travel to more places in a year than most people did in a lifetime.

But it was in Iceland that Billy came up against a problem he had never encountered anywhere before. Billy managed one of the smaller clubs in the hinterland and he used to tell me: 'When the snow was on the ground the only place we could practise was on the runway of the airfield. We used to have a kickabout on the tarmac, and when a plane approached we'd have a rest, wait until it had landed and then go on with the game again.'

One night though Billy and his team were due to play in Reykjavik, and as usual after a light training session Billy ordered the lads to bed for an afternoon's kip.

He was dozing in his own bed when there was a knock on the door and his young keeper ... a blond giant of a boy ... walked in and said: 'Boss, I've a problem.'

Billy, playing the fatherly figure, said: 'Come in lad. Sit down and let's discuss it ... it can't be all that bad.'

The keeper duly sat down on the edge of Billy's bed and admitted: 'The thing is boss ... I'm in love.'

Billy, sympathetic as ever, put an arm round his shoulders and offered some sage advice. 'Don't worry about that son ... we all fall in love at some time. The thing is enjoy it while you can. It's human nature.'

'That's true,' said the lad. 'Trouble is boss ... I'M IN LOVE WITH YOU!'

Billy was in a blind panic but didn't want

to blow a good run... and the keeper was a good 'un.

He thought for a moment and said: 'I tell you what – if you keep playing well until the end of the season we'll get engaged!' At the end of the season Billy was off like a shot... no doubt leaving a broken-hearted blond Viking behind!

4 GREAVSIE
MIRTH FROM THE MIDLANDS

For four years Jimmy Greaves has brought fun into football on ITV's networked Saint and Greavsie Show. *But Central viewers have enjoyed Jimmy's humour for much longer... it was Central Sport who gave Greavsie his big chance on television and he made Friday nights compulsive viewing with his forthright and hilarious views on football. Jimmy too had his laughs... at the humour of the Midlanders... and in this chapter he remembers some of the funny moments and characters from his time on telly in the area.*

When I was first approached to appear on Central Television as a so-called soccer expert (how I hate that term) on their Friday night sports programme I thought: 'Probably get a couple of months out of this and then get the hook.' Eight years later I'm still doing Central Sport and still getting a laugh out of it.

When I was a player, the Midlands was somewhere you boarded a bus to every other Saturday. It was not a place to stay, and because of that when I first appeared on Central Television I found it difficult to pick up the Brummie dialect and humour. It didn't take me long though to realise that Midlanders were every bit as funny as cheeky Cockneys, sharp Scousers or garrulous Glaswegians. When the laughter came through, Birmingham became my home from home.

Strangely the Midlands folk took to me too. That surprised me. After all, here was this London geezer going on about 'What's black and white and slides down tables?... Notts County!' I mean I deserved to be lynched. Instead the Midlanders accepted my patter for what it is – a tongue-in-cheek look at a game which at times takes itself far too seriously.

I know the knockers might say I take the mickey out of football... but I'll have this bet with any of the po-faced crowd who want to depress viewers with endless stories of crises, take-over bids and relegation struggles: the Saint and myself will tackle any particularly important football subject harder than they will come Saturday lunchtimes. Anyway, people should have a laugh. It happens in the dressing-rooms all the time. Why not transfer the behind-the-scenes humour to telly ... it seems to work you know.

Television, of course, has brought me into contact with many of the present-day 'media' managers, men who operated in the Central area, such as God himself, Brian Clough; the jewel in the crown of West Brom, Ron Atkinson; my one-time England Under-21 boss Joe Mercer and a host of other personalities who have convinced me that Midlands Mirth has a high place in any laughter league.

Cloughie, one of my old adversaries on Central on Friday nights, is, of course, a law unto himself. I mean, what kind of manager can regularly openly slag off his board of directors, including the chairman, and still be in a job years later?

I remember Brian when he was a sharp young centre forward with Middlesbrough ... and Brian remembers his talent well too.

He can have sharp words for any striker who gives even the remotest hint of rising above his station. I remember one match when Peter Withe, the man whose goal gave Aston Villa their European Cup Final win, scored a First Division hat-trick for Forest.

Most managers would have been delighted, but, at the compulsory Clough press conference after the match, Brian was asked if Big Peter had been presented with the match ball as a memento. 'No,' replied Cloughie. 'He'll get one when he learns to play with it.'

Since Peter Withe went on to play - and play well - for England, you gather from that that Mr Clough is no respecter of reputations. Mind you, few will forget Cloughie making a bit of a 'clown' of himself during the World Cup qualifying match with Poland at Wembley in 1973. He christened the Polish keeper Jan Tomasweski 'a clown' as he defied England's front line ... admittedly with some rather unorthodox saves. The big

Cloughie - no respecter of persons!

Pole, though, had the last laugh. His team beat us 1-0 and England went out of the tournament!

A few years later, Midlands viewers tittered when a bloke dressed in a clown's outfit was dragged off the pitch by Cloughie. Some television smart aleck commented 'Yes, but which one is the clown?' I wonder who that could have been?

Brian, of course, now has another star in the family ... young Nigel, his footballing son.

Nigel, to my mind is one of the most exciting young talents in today's game - how good to see him win the Barclays Young Eagle award last season - was almost ever present in England's Under-21 squad last season. I say almost, for he missed one vital

45

game – the Under-21 European Championship semi-final first leg with France. Nigel went down with chicken pox on the day of the match and prompted one of the best true stories I have heard in football.

Dave Sexton, who does a great job with our young players, was in charge of the squad, and when a doctor was called and chicken pox diagnosed he had to pull young Nigel out of the team.

A few minutes later Clough senior telephoned from England: 'Is Nigel in?' he asked Dave.

Dave, taken aback by the personal call (Brian doesn't call many people), stuttered 'No Brian, he's out… he's got chicken pox!'

After a moment of silence, Cloughie was soon blasting down the phone… enough to say that he wanted young Nigel to play and that chicken pox was not enough to keep him out of the team.

'Get the little ******* out of bed. He'll be all right. Make him play,' was the gist of the conversation. 'I'll phone back in half an hour.'

Dave, who naturally had wanted Nigel in the team in the first place, reconsulted the team doctor and asked 'Any way he can play?'

The Doc stood firm: 'It's a known medical fact that every year around eight per cent of athletes die when they play sport affected by a virus. My decision is that you cannot take the risk – he cannot play.'

Dave, suitably reassured, sat down to wait for the second phone call… two in a day from Cloughie was quite an occasion.

Sure enough on came Brian. 'Have you got him out of bed the little *******?' he enquired. 'No,' said Dave. 'Why not?' shouted Cloughie. 'Get him out of bed and play him. He'll be fine.'

Dave then patiently told Cloughie the story. 'Eight per cent of all athletes per year die by participating in sport while affected by a virus… the Doc says NO.'

There was silence at the other end of the telephone, then Cloughie muttered, 'I don't want the little **** to die.' And the line went dead.

Mind you, inside I know Cloughie must be deeply proud of his lad – there was a pleased look about him when Nigel was presented with his Young Eagle Trophy at Wembley before millions on ITV last spring.

And just before that, he did admit to Gary Newbon on Central Television that he was delighted with Nigel's progress last season. He stopped short though when Gary suggested that his son might even become a better striker than Cloughie was himself. 'Aye,' came the reply, 'and pigs might fly!'

Young Nigel, though, can look back with pride on last season. He was the first Forest striker for twenty years to score more than twenty goals in a season… and for me he is a certainty to gain full England honours.

Clough, of course, does like to have the last word, but now and again it doesn't happen.

Once during his early years at Derby County, Cloughie phoned from his office to the reserve team dressing-room and instructed a young apprentice to make him a cup of tea.

'Bugger off,' said the voice. 'Do you know who this is?' shrieked Cloughie. 'Yes – do you know who this is?' came the reply.

'No, I don't know,' boomed Cloughie. 'Well, you can definitely bugger off, then.' What an opportunist!

It's not only players who feel the sharp edge of Cloughie's wit. A couple of seasons

Young Nigel comes a cropper. Is he as good as his dad?

ago Forest were playing at Villa and Brian met Villa chairman Doug Ellis as he arrived at the ground. Doug was wearing a surgical collar and Cloughie went straight for the jugular. 'Good evening, Mr Chairman,' he said, 'I see the manager has finally got his own back!'

Deadly Doug Ellis... now there's a Midlands character to behold. It was me who christened Doug 'Deadly Doug' a few years back during my regular Friday evening spot on Central Television... and the nickname has stuck... even the ballboys at Villa Park call him Mr Deadly these days.

I think Doug secretly likes his notoriety... but he did take his revenge when he once invited me on a salmon-fishing trip on the glorious River Tay near Perth. After a couple of hours' instruction from the ghillie I actually caught my first salmon and 'Deadly' took great delight in 'blooding' me by daubing the entrails of the fish all over my forehead.

Totally unnecessary of course, and later that night I heard one of the waiters comment, 'Phew, have you had a whiff of Greavsie's aftershave?' I told him I got it from the Saint!

And there was worse to come. Being a mere beginner Doug conned me into believing that the best place to catch salmon on this particular stretch of river was from a small rock protruding from the middle of the fast-flowing water.

He rowed me to the rock, helped me onto it and then rowed away. I was finally rescued some time later after promising never to call him 'Deadly Doug' again. I did promise, but I've news for him... I was never in the Scouts!

Anyway, it seems that now Doug has Graham Taylor as manager at Villa Park he doesn't need me to keep him in line!

Two men who always make me laugh are big Ron Atkinson and the old Bald Eagle himself... Jim Smith.

Now it so happens that this pair of characters are also the greatest of mates, and when they get together the one-liners fly as quick as they did between Bob Hope and Bing Crosby.

Big Ron is one of football's great characters and also one of its fairest men. The press have labelled Ron as something of a Flash Harry figure... but it's just not true. Watch *Spitting Image* or read certain tabloid newspapers and you would imagine that the man went about dripping gold and swallowing champagne by the bucketful. Truth be told the only bit of gold I've seen on Ron's wrist is his wrist watch. And while champagne was always on order at his post-match press conferences at Old Trafford when he managed Manchester United the big fellow used to settle for a cup of tea. In fact, if I was there it was tea for two!

And one thing about the big guy. He was always on hand to face the press, win or lose. He was not one of those managers who are all smiles and quotes when their team wins, but nowhere to be seen when they lose.

Ron's wit, though, is as sharp as his dress... and believe me that's pretty sharp. And when he and Jim Smith get into their act it is hilarious.

During Ron's first spell at West Brom, Jim was manager at Birmingham, and whenever they were together it was a laugh a minute.

Usually it was Jim playing Wise to Ron's Morecambe. Like the time they were waiting for the lift at the Royal Garden Hotel in Kensington. The doors opened, the lift attendant said 'Going down?' 'He is,' replied Atkinson.

Ron always reckoned that Jim only signed

FA Cup semi-final
Steve Chettle brings down John Barnes conceding a penalty to Liverpool *(left)*, and *(above)* John Aldridge scores the goal which denied Forest a Wembley place against Wimbledon . . . and Greavsie tipping a double!

the Argentinian Alberto Tarantini because he thought he'd got eight legs, and even casual conversations with third parties would be used to remind Jim that Birmingham were struggling and West Brom were riding high.

Billy Connolly had been appearing at Birmingham Hippodrome, and after the show Ron and Jim bumped into the Scottish comedian at Andy Gray's nightclub. They congratulated him on a great show and Billy remarked how good the audience had been, adding: 'I love playing Birmingham.' 'Doesn't everybody?' asked Ron.

Atkinson hardly needed any help with his one-liners - but there was another willing ally in Albion's midfield player Len Cantello. It was during the freeze-up in the middle of the 1979-80 season, when Albion were challenging at the top of the First Division and Birmingham were at the bottom. Neither team had played for a couple of weeks so the managers fixed up a challenge match in snow-less Guernsey and a local paper put up the 'Arctic Cup' for the winners. The teams flew together from Birmingham airport in a rickety old Viscount, and just after take-off the passenger cabin suddenly went completely silent as the plane hit turbulence and dropped about 200 feet. Words of re-assurance were needed, and they came from Cantello. 'Don't worry, lads,' he said, 'Birmingham won't go down twice in one season.' Mind you, Smithy had the last laugh - they beat Albion and won the Arctic Cup.

There are not many cups in Birmingham's trophy room - but their fans treat failure with a rare sense of humour. Two of my favourite quips from the St Andrews terraces are: 'Oh well, you draw some and lose some', and 'We've done the double - stayed up twice.'

My very favourite is from the last time they called the insurance assessor in to revalue the trophies. The bloke opened the cupboard and out jumped Lord Lucan.

Smithy, though, has a marvellous sense of humour and really he has to have with the stick he gets about that shining pate of his. Saint reckons Jim doesn't keep a comb in his inside pocket... just some Johnson's polish.

Seriously though, Jim is a smashing football character and I reckon the job he did at Queen's Park Rangers last season, finishing the league in fifth spot and as top London club, was nothing short of miraculous.

Coventry City is another Midlands club which has always had a sense of humour.

When Joe Mercer was general manager in the late 1970s, they were beaten 7-0 by a West Brom team featuring the black players Laurie Cunningham, Cyrille Regis and Brendon Batson. Afterwards Joe comforted team manager Gordon Milne with the words: 'It could have been worse - we might have been playing them at cricket.'

The tradition has been carried on recently by the partnership of managing director George Curtis and manager John Sillett - my old mate from as far back as Chelsea.

When Coventry were preparing for the semi-final FA Cup match with Leeds in 1987, they set up training headquarters at a Dorset hotel. One night the lads decided to hold a 'silly shirt and tie' competition, and, just as judging was being done by Central Television sport reporter Bob Hall, in walked Sillett wearing a black wig on his bald head, dark glasses, an outrageous shirt and 1960s kipper tie, loud Bermuda shorts and beach sandals. He was quite offended when it was announced he'd won the competition and reckoned that was how he normally dressed when he was relaxing. Coventry's central defender Trevor Peake climaxed the evening by presenting John with a bottle of mineral water and announcing that he'd just been named 'Perrier Manager of the Month'.

Sill turned up in the wig again when I was doing a live outside broadcast from Coventry's eve of Cup Final hotel in Marlow. He threatened to throw me in the Thames, but I warned that if he did I would tip Coventry to beat Spurs the following day – and they regarded that as a fate worse than death.

Throughout their Cup run, Coventry's players had gone out of their way to make sure I would tip against them in the Cup which I did from the third round onwards. Every time a feature was done on Coventry's Cup run by Central Sport or the *Saint and Greavsie Show,* skipper Brian Kilcline would pop up at the end and beg me to keep tipping against them.

That's why Sill shouted up a thank-you message to me in the commentary box as he was swaggering around Wembley with the Cup after Coventry's extra time victory over Spurs.

By the way, I'm still waiting on the boss's bonus for tipping two FA Cup winners on the trot... and both big outsiders too.

To be fair, I did have two bites at the Cup cherry last season as I went for Nottingham Forest and Wimbledon to contest the final. Forest only fell to Liverpool in the semi, so I wasn't far away. Probably the combination of Cloughie never having made an FA Cup Final and me tipping them proved too much of a burden.

So far the only congratulatory letters I've had are from those champagne and cigar boys the bookies... it appears that every time I tip one team the punters go for the opposition. Their satchels were bulging after the Wombles spoiled the Liverpool party.

Cyrille Regis getting the better of Leeds United in the 1987 FA Cup semi-final

We've given Tommy Docherty his head elsewhere in the book and no-one can tell Doc stories better than the old boy himself, but no 'Midlands Mirth' chapter would be complete without one classic tale involving the Doc. The day Tommy arrived to take over as manager of Derby County, the man he was replacing, manager Colin Murphy, and assistant manager Dario Gradi, were waiting at the Baseball Ground to find out their fate. Doc eventually called Colin into his office and when he returned he told Dario: 'It's good news and bad news, mate. The good news is he's offered me a job – the bad news is he's offered me your job.'

Another Derby manager was my old Spurs team-mate Dave Mackay. The day after a local reporter had written a particularly scathing attack on Dave's team in his newspaper column, he was summoned to Dave's office to be told: 'I never read your crap – but this time you've gone too far.'

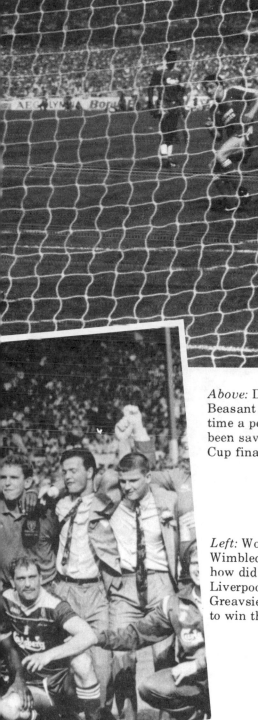

Above: Dave Beasant – the first time a penalty has been saved in a Cup final

Left: Wonderful Wimbledon. Just how did they beat Liverpool, and Greavsie's tipping, to win the Cup?

The evening before West Bromwich Albion's FA Cup semi-final with Leicester City in 1969, manager Alan Ashman had imposed a curfew at the team's hotel in Southport. But a couple of the players must have felt the need for a nightcap to settle their nerves because, on his way to his bedroom, Ashman bumped into a waiter carrying a tray containing a pint of lager and a rum and Coke. Ashman confiscated the tray, discovered the identity of the recipients from the waiter, and calmly knocked on their bedroom door. 'Drinks, gentlemen,' he called. 'Come in,' they replied. Ashman walked in with his tray and announced: 'Here are your drinks, gentlemen. That'll be £250 each.'

Another former Albion manager was Jimmy Hagan, and when he left the Hawthorns he had a very successful time in charge of the top Portuguese team, Benfica in Lisbon. When Jim eventually returned to England he was asked why Benfica were always so successful in Portugal. 'Simple,' he said, 'they have the best players, the best stadium, the best training facilities and the best referees.'

On the subject of referees – a final word from Ron Atkinson. After West Brom had been beaten 1-0 by Red Star in Belgrade in the UEFA Cup following a dubious decision by an East German referee, Ron was asked what he thought of the official. 'It has always been my policy not to comment on referees,' he replied, 'and I'm certainly not making an exception for this idiot.'

So Midlands football has a lot to offer in the laughter line, but as an appendix I'm not letting my mates at Central Sport get away scot-free after what they've put me through over the years.

The two main culprits are Gary Newbon and Jeff Farmer. Gary Newbon, a legend in

his own mind, doubles up as sports presenter and Head of Sport, Central Television... now there's an anomaly for you. Mind you, Gary enjoys it. He's often to be seen looking in the mirror in his office saying to himself 'I thought you were wonderful last night mate.'

Gary's right-hand man and my editor at Central is Jeff Farmer, a former newspaper sports writer who tried his luck at telly. And truth be told he doesn't seem to have much luck at anything else... particularly with those three-legged nags he keeps tipping me.

Together over the years they have concocted some marvellous assignments for me, like the time they got me hang-gliding... and I nearly broke my ruddy neck.

Game for anything I am. What they didn't tell me was the 'orrible things come down faster than they go up. I was left hanging like the Bird Man of Broad Street as I plummeted to the ground thinking, 'Well at least I tasted the glamour of television before I died.' Funny how producers never actually do the stunts themselves isn't it?

Top: Alan Ashman congratulates his West Bromwich Albion team following the 1969 FA Cup final win against Everton – but did he cancel the fines?

Above: Jimmy Hagan – Portuguese referees were not his favourites

And I've got news for those two characters... I'm going to reveal to the world how they ruined the careers of three great sports stars.

You see Gary and Jeff (or the dynamic duo as they are known to themselves) thought it would be a great idea to put me in with some of the superstars of sport... people like Tracy Austin, the wonder girl of world tennis, Seve

54

Ballesteros, the matador of world golf, and another tennis great, John McEnroe.

Trouble is they hadn't thought of my reputation. While the interviews and matches went well enough, it was a case of Jim'll Jinx It for the talented trio.

Since I had my audience with them, McEnroe has never won a top tennis tournament, Seve took four years to win another major, and worst of all Tracy has never played again.

Gary and Jeff blame me, of course, but all good producers should do their homework - after all, my tipping record has not been the greatest over the years. I blame the guilty men... Newbon and Farmer... all lack of earnings claims should go to them c/o Central Television.

5 A VISIT FROM THE DOC

The Doc at Altrincham – showing another
Chairman the way?

No book of football humour would be complete without a contribution from Tommy Docherty. The Doc, like Shankly, is one of life's unbeatable characters. He has been a friend of mine from my early days as a Scottish International and his infectious fun-loving style has put a smile on the face of soccer. A cork on a stormy soccer sea on many occasions, he has a joke for every occasion and for every club. Here the Doc takes us through his football career . . . with anecdotes all the way.

When I was first approached to contribute to this book I had two questions to ask and one observation to make. 'Who's it for?', 'What do Saint and Greavsie want with me?' and, 'Is that all I'm being paid!' Eventually we agreed that I'd receive for my efforts a case of Ron Atkinson bubble bath. Or, as we know it, Dom Perignon champagne.

I'm sure that most people nowadays regard me as an after dinner speaker who, as a football manager, had more clubs than Jack Nicklaus, but let's start with the early days. Growing up as a child in Glasgow.

My first two football clubs were St Paul's Boys' Guild and St Mark's school team. Like most kids in Glasgow at that time, we kicked anything that moved. A piece of rag, a tin can, the opposing players and, on occasions, each other.

Unfortunately, there was no organised schoolboy football as there is today. No England or Scotland youth teams. No Ian St John soccer camps, which help the kids enormously, although it must be frustrating for the Saint having a ten-year-old run rings round him.

As a kid, I used to play two matches every Saturday. St Mark's in the morning and the Boys' Guild in the afternoon, the latter being a Catholic team run by the church. In those days we feared only two people, the priest and the Glasgow police, in that order. Although we respected our local Bobby, Father Joseph Connolly held far more terror. I still consider those to be the best years of my footballing career. Come to think of it, so do a lot of people.

Everyone's ambition was to play for the team you supported, which in my case, being a Catholic, was Celtic. Someone asked me recently if I'd always been a Catholic. I said, 'Yes, until I saw *The Thorn Birds* a few years ago.' On the other hand, if you were a Protestant, then your ambition was to play for Rangers. Of course there was great bigotry then. Your parents, right or wrong, brought you up a good Catholic with Celtic on a Saturday and Mass on a Sunday. But even though we took great delight in watching our heroes, we always preferred playing. Most common were inter-street games, you with your green shirts and the opposition wearing blue; games which were played with more fervour than many top teams I've been associated with.

Like most kids, we were always in trouble:

smashing windows, up in court for playing football in the street (the Old Bailey wasn't my first appearance before a Judge), which wouldn't happen these days - one reason being that our modern roads are so congested with cars that it would be near impossible.

I remember Celtic opening their gates for early leavers with about twenty minutes to go. This enabled us kids to nip in and watch the end of a game free of charge. I'm sure many a club nowadays keeps them locked so the supporters can't get out!

After watching Celtic it was straight home, a quick tea, change and out wearing the guise of your hero. In my case it was Malcolm McDonald. Not the 'Super Mac' of recent years but THE Malcolm McDonald, later manager of Brentford who went on to manage Scotland.

I was the captain of St Paul's, which in turn was run by the priest. Needless to say, if you didn't go to Mass you were automatically dropped, no matter how good a player you were. This gave me an extra responsibility as captain. Not only was I to lead my team, but I also had to get them out of bed on Sunday morning to attend Holy Communion. And, mark my words, ensuring that George Best turned up for a training session was nothing compared to those cold winter Sunday mornings knocking up your best players and dragging them off to early Mass.

As for my family, my father, who was a foundry worker, died when I was eight, so I never knew that much about him. My mother brought us up in relative poverty, more than making up for his loss. She was a very hard woman, probably due to the difficult times she suffered, but she had great strength and character. She never missed a game or the chance to admonish a wayward referee. Of course, being a very bigoted lady, she had no time for Protestants. Even less for the English. So I shudder to think what she'd make of the English Protestants now playing in Scotland.

I turned out for the Boys' Guild until I was seventeen and a half. This was a difficult time to get a job, especially in football, because it meant you were only six months short of your National Service. So, instead, I signed for Shettleston Juniors. Shettleston played in one of the toughest leagues I've ever experienced. Some of their players made Tommy Smith look like Wayne Sleep! So it was just as well I was rescued by the army three months later or I might never have made it to professional level.

National Service is something the youngsters of today wouldn't know about. I was in the H.L.I., 'Hitler's last issue'. Actually, it was Palestine with the Highland Light

Infantry. During my army career I played lots of football alongside people like Arthur Rowley, the Football League's most prolific goalscorer, Adam Little of Rangers and Ken Bowyer of Stoke. A number of people I was involved with began writing to football clubs recommending they give me a trial. When I left the army I had the choice of signing for Newcastle or Burnley, possibly even Manchester United, had I been good enough, which would have been ironic. That has been something I've thought about since, because, had circumstances been different, I could have been involved in the Munich air disaster. I would have been thirty years of age in 1958. Older, but experienced, and, had I been able to hold a place in that exceptional team, who knows what might have happened.

I well remember that fateful day. I was playing for Preston North End and was driving back from a training session at Standish when I saw the billboard. At first I couldn't believe it and thought it was some sick publicity stunt. I stopped to buy a paper and was hit by the full horror. Soon afterwards United tried to sign a number of players as replacements for the lads who'd perished in the crash. I was one of them. But Cliff Britton, the Preston manager, refused to sell me to another local club.

My first signing after leaving the army was for Celtic in 1948. At last I realised my boyhood dream. Unfortunately, a lad called Bobby Evans occupied the same position as me. He was a dynamic wing-half who prevented me getting into the team. Except, of course, when he was injured or playing for Scotland.

About a year later the chairman, Mr Bob Kelly, sent for me and told me I was being transferred to Preston North End for £3000 because he felt I wouldn't make the grade at Celtic. Obviously I was bitterly disappointed by this and asked the reason why. Did he not think me good enough? To which he said, 'No, you're not big enough!' I left that week. The following week they signed Bobby Collins, who, incidentally, was about ten inches shorter than me!

As big a disappointment as leaving Celtic was the fact I was leaving Glasgow, which I loved. But things improved when I arrived at Preston North End because I found myself in great company - names that live on today. People like Tom Finney, who I reckon to be the greatest player of all time. Who also, like most other players then, was qualified in a trade. Tom was in the plumbing business so we were christened 'The plumber and the ten leaks'.

The great Tom Finney - but where are the ten leaks?

This is where the modern game differs. People harp on about players being over-paid, but in my opinion it's a short career which could easily be ended prematurely by a misjudged or badly timed tackle. So I say good luck to the players of today. Get what you can out of the game because I can assure you it doesn't last long.

But back to Tom Finney. Clubs in those days were never in financial difficulties because their pay was on a sliding scale. In my case the slide was downwards. The absolute maximum you could earn then was fourteen pounds a week. Fourteen pounds! I've paid more than that for a cigar. Tom Finney was on the maximum all year round. I was on fourteen pounds in the winter but dropped to eight pounds in the summer. As you can imagine this was disastrous. It wasn't bad money for doing nothing, but unfortunately it wasn't enough to live on.

The following year I got my tenth cap for Scotland against England at Wembley, so I went to see Bill Scott, who was then the manager. I asked him for the same deal of fourteen pounds throughout the year. He said, 'But you're not as good a player as Finney.' I replied, 'I am during the summer.' Eventually I got the same as Finney, and looking back it was a marvellous ten years at the club. In fact, I truly believed I would see my playing career out with Preston.

Preston was also the place where I first met Bill Shankly. Unfortunately, as I joined the club Bill was on his way to manage Workington after a distinguished playing career. Of course that wasn't the last I heard of him. Apart from his well-documented success I also had ten years of marvellous Shanks stories told religiously before games on Saturday.

This brings me to a pet subject of mine. Along with Saint, I believe there were a lot more characters in the game in those days. More so than now.

I was soon to realise my playing career would not end at Preston when I was transferred to Arsenal on 14 August 1958 for £30,000. I spent three years at Highbury, but can honestly say that nothing funny ever happened to me there. On or off the pitch! Unusual for me. Highbury was a cross between my National Service days and West Point. There were four club rules. You had to wear good clothes, have your hair cut, shave every day, and present a good image for the club. I don't know how George Best would have coped because he'd only qualify for one of the four.

The players I was associated with at Arsenal read like an International Gallery of Fame: Jimmy Bloomfield (England), Vic Groves (England), David Herd (Scotland), Jack Kelsey (Welsh goalkeeper), Joe Harvey (Republic of Ireland), Arthur Knott (England and also a great cricketer), David Bowen (Wales), and Jackie Henderson.

The end came when I attained the ripe old age of thirty-two. I had always intended to retire at the top and not to play out my career in the lower divisions, so I applied for a coaching job at Chelsea in 1962 along with Jimmy Adamson. At the time it was reckoned that we were two of the best up and coming coaches in the game and Jim would have got the job before me if it hadn't been for his desire to continue playing. As for me, I was finished, even though I did play one or two games. I went for an interview with the Chairman, Joe Mears, who was a marvellous man. Joe was very encouraging and said to me, 'Tom, you're no doubt aware that we're looking for a coach.' I replied, 'I saw the game last Saturday Mr Chairman and believe me, it's not a coach you need, it's a hearse!'

Tommy – still sticking his chin out, even in Chelsea days

Then he said something which encouraged me even more. He said, 'Tom, I'm the Chairman of the club. I know nothing about football.' Which was very refreshing. Then he added, 'And the other five here know a damn sight less.' Now this must be unique. A chairman admitting he knows nothing about football! For this reason I respected the man and still believe if he hadn't died I wouldn't have had eighteen clubs. I wouldn't have been manager of Scotland or Manchester United either. I'd be manager of Chelsea.

But unfortunately for the club, and me, Mr Mears died and was succeeded by a man named Bill Pratt. Yes, that was his name and we all know the old saying. This man had been a chairman for twenty-five years and *still* knew nothing. Needless to say we fell out at our first board meeting, when I said to him, 'Mr Chairman, when I want your advice I'll give it to you.' A week later I

was on my way out of Chelsea.

But we had seven great years. I had taken over a side that was dead. But we had Dick Foss as youth team manager and a chief scout called Jimmy Tompson, who was the best. There were no rules about schoolboys in those days so he didn't have to break any. He captured the best in the south. Players like Venables, Bonetti, the two Harrises, Mel Scott. Unbelievable when you consider how much talent one man could amass. So all I did in effect when I became manager was to give them a chance.

I could see the future of youth. When I arrived there on 22 February 1962, Chelsea had already been relegated with Ted Drake as manager. I got the job on a Thursday and had to report to Stamford Bridge on the Saturday where we were to play Blackpool. As it happens the score was 2–2. But when I arrived, Mr Drake, who was a very nice man, was waiting for me.

He said, 'I just want you to know, Tom, that you weren't my choice. I wanted Vic Buckingham.'

Understandable seeing as he and Vic had been in the RAF together. I replied, 'Thank you Mr Drake. That's very kind of you to tell me.' At least with a man like Ted Drake you knew where you stood.

When I first arrived at Chelsea a certain young player called ...? hang on I'll remember it in a second... er? ... Jimmy Greaves, that's it – had already signed to go to Milan so there was nothing I could do about it. But even in those days you could see he was something special.

One look at the side told you it wasn't the youngest in the country. Ted Drake, gentleman as he was, tended to run things with his heart and not his head. At the end of that season he was sacked and I took over as caretaker manager until Christmas.

Greavsie at Chelsea – the Doc just missed him

The following month of January saw me appointed as team manager and my first game was against, you've guessed it, Liverpool. And yes, the Saint was playing.

That was the start of some great years at Stamford Bridge. We won the League Cup, now the Littlewoods Cup, we won promotion back to the First Division in our first season. We were never out of the top three in the First Division all the time I was there. We lost in the Cup Final of 1967 to Tottenham 3–1. A Spurs side that boasted two ex-Chelsea players – Terry Venables and that dreaded Jimmy Greaves. The Burke and Hare of football.

Having said that, we had some great players ourselves during that time. I remember Bill Shankly saying to Bob Paisley

that we were the one team Liverpool were concerned about. Not afraid, because Shanks was fearless, but that didn't stop him showing some concern, and I take that as a compliment to our great young side.

Then, as I've mentioned, the Chairman died and it was only a matter of time before I went to Rotherham. The year was 1967, and Rotherham was a lovely little club which suited me. Mainly because they only had three directors, two of them being from the same family. Eric Purshouse and his son Lewis.

The only mistake I made was promising I'd take them out of the Second Division. I did. I took them into the Third. But we did get through to the fifth round of the FA Cup that year. Three teams had qualified for Wembley and we were due to play Leicester City on the Saturday at home. We drew one each so went for the replay on the Tuesday at Leicester and lost 2–1 in extra time.

On the Sunday before the match I had the players down at the ground. I lined them up on the pitch and began introducing them to an old chap wearing a bowler hat. The old Chairman came down and asked what I was doing. I said, 'Well Mr Chairman, I'm getting the lads used to Wembley so that when they meet the King they won't be nervous.' He said, 'But it's the Queen at Wembley.' I said, 'I know. But by the time we get there it'll be the King again!'

It was a great little club and at one time the players were on a bonus system. Twenty-five pounds for a win! A lot of money then. It got so bad that whenever our lads pushed up past the half-way line, the Chairman would stand up and shout, 'Offside ref!'

Then we come to Queen's Park Rangers, where I got my famous hat-trick. I was appointed manager three times! Somebody asked me once if I'd ever won the 'Manager of the Month' at Q.P.R. I said, 'No, I wasn't there a month.' In 1968 I lasted twenty-eight days, although I did receive a miniature bottle for 'Bell's Manager of the Week'. More of Q.P.R. later.

My next appointment was Aston Villa with a Chairman called Doug Ellis. You could count on Doug... usually to upset things. Once he said to me, 'Don't worry Tom, I'm behind you.' I said, 'I don't want you behind me, I want you in front of me where I can see you!'

Doug Ellis is reputed to have rung up the Prime Minister of Israel and said, 'I want to be buried in the same place as Jesus.' The Prime Minister said, 'That'll cost you a million pounds.' Doug replied, 'That's a lot for three days.'

What an ego the man had. But I must say this for him, he was always about the place. Usually in the way, but always about. It was Greavsie who christened him Deadly Doug. For once he got something right!

After my exit from Villa in 1969 I flew off to Portugal to join Oporto. There was never any problem with the club apart from the language difficulty. They couldn't understand me. The Chairman said, 'Mr Docherty, we want you to learn Portuguese before the end of next year.' I said, 'Fine. So long as I can learn English before the end of this one.'

The main advantage of managing in Portugal is that out there you are employed as a coach. You're there to manage and pick the team. The day-to-day running of the club, including transfers and finance, is left to the Chairman and board. This proved an excellent system. In fact, some English clubs are adopting similar tactics over here. Take Liverpool, for example. John Smith and Peter Robinson sign the players that Kenny wants. The main advantage being that the manager has an excellent relationship with the players while his relationship with the Chairman is never allowed to become strained.

Oporto was a wonderful time for me. But as usual in my career I soon found it time to move on. So from one fishing port to another, I landed in Hull as assistant manager to Terry Neill.

Hull City, home of the fishing fleet, with one or two prawns on the board. Again, contrary to popular belief, I found myself in the company of a wonderful Chairman, Harold Needler. I was grateful to Terry for getting me back into the English game because once you have been working out of the country it's more difficult to get back in. By that I don't mean back into the country, but back into sport. Although one or two cricketers have experienced trouble in both.

Terry did a fantastic job at the club and we found ourselves in the unusual position of Terry as player-manager and me as coach.

This was highlighted during a pre-season friendly game against the Japanese national eleven side. We had an agreement that I'd concentrate on training and coaching and Terry would implement my ideas as manager with the team on the pitch.

During this particular game we were winning 8-0, but, even so, Terry wasn't keeping his part of the bargain and was having a poor game. Twenty minutes from the end I decided he had to be substituted. This proved a problem, because on the pitch I had the authority, but once Terry had completed his bath and changed back into his suit he once again adopted his role of manager. Needless to say, we could smile about the event afterwards, which is just as well. I wasn't to spend much longer at the club, but it could have been even shorter after my ill-timed substitution.

I spent an enjoyable six months at Hull helping Terry Neill, then along came the Scottish offer in 1970. I followed Bobby Brown to manage my national side. In fact, I had the great honour of playing for, captaining, and managing my country. Only a handful of people have done this in the history of football. Danny Blanchflower played, captained and managed Ireland. Terry Yorath played and captained Wales. Bobby Robson, well, he's had a few games for England hasn't he?

But back to Scotland. I had players like Denis Law, who was coming to the end of his career. There was also a young lad to whom I gave his first cap. His name was Kenny Dalglish. Whatever happened to him?

One player who was never included in my squad was the Saint. Mind you, it was 1970, and at the age of forty-six, the Saint very wisely called it a day.

I remember a game we played against Denmark where Kenny and Joe Harper were substitutes. There were about twenty minutes to go and I told Joe to get warmed up. He then decided he wanted to use the toilet which, as you can appreciate, isn't the ideal time. I told him to make sure he was quick about it. Ten minutes later Joe was still missing. Suddenly I heard a banging noise on a big gate a few yards away from the touchline. It transpired that while Joe was out relieving himself someone had come along and closed the gates. So poor Joe only managed five minutes in his first international instead of twenty!

This brings us to 1972, possibly the most documented part of my career as a football manager.

I knew I'd been chosen for the job at Old Trafford when I saw the white smoke coming out of the boardroom window. To become the manager of United must be one of the most prestigious, sought-after positions, not only in this country, but in the world. I always felt, from early on, that I was destined for that job.

Again, there were some wonderful characters. A young lad I signed called Gerry Daly – no, he wasn't a German newspaper as some would have us believe. Young Gerry is the only player I know to score a penalty while being filmed on *Match of the Day* and miss it the night it was shown!

As you may have gathered, the main thing you need to work in football, besides skill and dedication, is a sense of humour. I bore the brunt of many a jibe from visiting supporters. Anfield, as I'm sure the Saint will bear out, is a great collection of Liverpool humour which can suddenly turn into one voice, dismissing any pretensions a

visiting manager may have.

You also need a sense of humour to play football! I remember we had Paddy Roche as goalkeeper. He was nicknamed 'the crocus' because he only came out once a year. Another name we had for him was 'Dracula', because he didn't like crosses.

I remember signing a big lad called Jim Holton from Shrewsbury for £80,000. Harry Gregg, who sold Jim to us, said, 'Tom, this lad doesn't know the meaning of the word defeat!' I phoned Harry back next week and said, 'Harry. It's not the only word he doesn't know the meaning of!'

With Manchester United I lost the FA Cup to Southampton in 1976 and won it against Liverpool the following year. The Liverpool match was refereed by Clive Thomas, who'd had more bookings that year than Thomas Cook. Not only did we bring the FA Cup to Old Trafford, but in the process had stopped Liverpool winning that famous treble of League, FA Cup and European Cup. I was delighted for us but felt sorry for Liverpool.

Of course, during my time at Old Trafford I had George Best as a member of my team. Georgie has gained some notoriety for being a difficult player. People often ask me if I had any trouble handling George. But I can honestly say I didn't. Mainly because he was never there!

One opinion I still hold about United is that at times, like Ted Drake at Chelsea, the club has been ruled from the heart and not the head. Players who should have been replaced by younger blood were often kept on by the club, which is sound in principle but does not make for success.

Regardless of Liverpool's achievements I still consider Manchester United to be the biggest club in the country and one of the most desirable to manage.

In 1977 my five-year association with the club was ended. The circumstances have been well publicised so we'll move straight on to Derby County.

Peter Osgood and Southampton prove the
masters in the 1976 FA Cup final

Both my predecessors, Brian Clough and
Dave Mackay, had won the championship,
but the team I inherited was an ageing one.
New blood was required. Unfortunately,
Brian Clough had moved to Brighton with
his brilliant young son Nigel, who was then
just a babe. I would dearly have loved to
have signed a Clough, but in those days the
only one available was Frank Clough, the
golfing correspondent for the *Sun*. For-
tunately for me he wasn't available.

Derby was a steady period in my life,
where we never won anything but weren't
relegated.

Then it was back to Queen's Park Rangers
for the second time.

I brought in players like Clive Allen and
Paul Goddard. I knew Clive was a good kid
who'd go on to great things and he's since
proved me right.

Two other players I bought were Tony

contract, rise in salary. So I entered Jim's office full of confidence to find the champagne flowing. Jim left the office saying he'd be back in ten minutes, so I helped myself to a glass of bubbly. Jim eventually returned, toasted me and said, 'Well Tom, I think it's the parting of the ways.' I said, 'Don't go Mr Chairman, I think you're doing a grand job.' He replied, 'I'm not going Tom. You are. You're sacked.'

The players were up in arms over my dismissal and Jim immediately climbed down saying there'd been a mistake. Did Tommy Docherty say a Chairman had admitted making a mistake? Yes. I was re-engaged, but later that summer Jim Gregory saved face and sacked me again!

So off I went to make way for Terry Venables. Luckily during this time I'd bought a caravan, which was handy for moving the family from job to job. In fact we had two jobs and a fortnight's holiday in the one month!

And now for something completely different. The year is 1981 and we set off for Australia. A place of great size and beauty. You can travel miles without seeing a single soul, which, unfortunately, is also true of their football stadiums. You'll find Aussie football supporters are the salt of the earth... that's if you can find one!

Currie and Stan Bowles. Now Stan did acquire a reputation as a gambler. In fact, someone said if Stan could pass a betting shop like he passed a ball then he'd be a rich man. But I honestly never had the slightest trouble with Stan.

In fact we were going very well, we'd just beaten Burnley 7-0 and were top of the Second Division. My contract had just expired, which is most unusual for me, when the Chairman, Jim Gregory, sent for me. I thought, this is it. Successful club, new

I took over Sydney Olympic football club on a part-time basis. One main difference between Aussie grounds and ours is that over there you have to move the sheep off the pitch before the match can start. In fact, some Aussie clubs might win more matches by leaving the sheep on! As for Sydney, support was so low that we announced the crowd changes to the team!

I've never understood why Big Ron Atkinson never went out there. He'd have loved it. He could have watched the game and got a suntan at the same time.

The team was predominantly Greek. In fact there were nine Greeks and two English. The Chairman insisted on buying two more Greek players, but I insisted I wanted English. Shortly after he was going round at a match collecting signatures. I asked him what it was for and he told me it was a petition for my resignation. I said, 'Bring it over here and I'll sign it myself.' Needless to say I was soon on my way back to England and a contract with Preston.

The great Tom Finney was President, I was returning to the club I'd spent so many happy years at. What could go wrong? I was sacked after four months.

So it was back to Australia. In fact I spent more time on that plane than I did at Preston North End!

South Melbourne was the club and a new long-term contract of six months. Well, it's long term for me! In fact it should have been nine months but the Chairman gave me three months off for good behaviour.

From there it was a short hop back over to Sydney Olympic. Just as well we never won the Australian Cup because being Greek they'd probably have smashed it on the floor and danced on it. I loved Australia. People were polite and during my time there I did some reporting and a spell on TV.

Then to Wolves. A great club of the past. Associated with great names like Stan Cullis, Derek Dougan, the Beverly Sisters. Some notable supporters too. The most famous one is Nick Owen, and, until recently, the only one!

I well remember an early press conference when a reporter said, 'I believe you intend doing for Wolves what J. F. Kennedy did for America.' I said, 'But he got shot!' The reporter had no need to reply.

One player we tried to sign was George Best. Unfortunately he'd gone missing. Miss America, Miss Jamaica.

Now we finally come to the end of my managerial career. Altrincham had always been one of my ambitions, or so I told them at the interview. I went there with the same intentions as I had in writing this chapter. To prove that money isn't everything.

I had gone to a non-league side. At around about the same time Ron Atkinson went to West Brom. I did hope that one day our sides would meet in the Vauxhall league, but that will never happen now, seeing as I've left Altrincham. And with it my last appointment. In fact, the only appointment I've had since was with a doctor over a bout of pleurisy.

Non-league football was a lot different from my time at bigger clubs. For a start, there was no clock in the ground. But I always knew when it was nearing half-time because the players would start edging their way over to the dugout. Money wasn't plentiful, but, to be fair to Altrincham, they did give me a sponsored car with a fantastic heated rear window. At least they ensured that your hands didn't get cold when you were pushing it.

On the subject of money, something else I found different there was the sponsorship. Our sponsor wanted maximum exposure so we had their name written across the back of the goalie's shorts.

The players were keen, but fitness was always a problem. I knew our right back wasn't good enough when I saw him going on an overlap at twenty past three and he made his way back at twenty past four. This was reflected in the vast number of players we went through. I signed so many that at the end of my pre-match pep talk I'd say, 'Right lads, best of luck, whoever you are.' Then add, 'I want you to do something you've never done before. Play well.'

Since leaving Altrincham I have been

offered the job at Maine Road, but my doctor told me to keep as far away from football as possible. Which brings me to the end of the Tommy Docherty story. I'm still involved in football through TV panels and my weekly show with Radio Piccadilly.

If I want the latest news I can always watch my favourite Saturday football show. Bob Wilson does a fantastic job!

Last of all, thanks to Saint and Greavsie for asking me to write this piece. Although I don't know how they ever understood it because the original submission was in joined-up writing.

I'm out of football but still smiling. Let's hope some of those still involved in the game can manage the odd smile as well.

6 SAINT A DISH OF SCOUSE

Liverpool has been my home for almost thirty years now and I can honestly say that in all that time I have never stopped marvelling at the humour of Merseyside.

Liverpudlians, like Cockneys and Glaswegians, are endowed with a quickfire wit and sense of fun which can only have been gifted by God. And I know that that sense of fun has spilled over from the terracings onto the pitches and into the dressing-rooms of Goodison and Anfield, creating an atmosphere which can be as valuable as a twelfth man on the pitch to Everton and Liverpool during a season.

Great gags abound. Like the famous one about a Reds supporter who spent so much time at Anfield his wife rounded on him one day saying: 'At times I think you love Liverpool more than you love me.' He looked at her wryly and countered: 'I tell you what... I love Everton more than I love you!'

Then there was the time when Everton were playing in a big European Cup Winners Cup tie. The two Blues supporters were waiting in the queue when one turned to the other and said, 'Bill, you'll never believe it but I've left the two tickets on the sideboard.' 'Don't worry,' said Bill. 'You hold our places and give me your key. I'll be back in ten minutes.'

Bill duly arrived at Tom's house and let himself in only to find Tom's wife in bed with the lodger. He grabbed the two tickets and slipped quietly away without being discovered.

He arrived back at Goodison just before Bill got to the turnstiles, handed over the tickets, and said: 'Tom I've bad news for you... your Missus is in bed with the lodger.'

Tom fixed him with a worried look and countered: 'I've got worse news for you mate... Andy Gray's not playing!'

Funny... and probably true!

One true story I still chuckle about concerns a Liverpool fan who had injured himself while working in Birmingham and was installed in a Birmingham hospital.

All was well until the Reds were due to play Villa. That was it, the Reds supporter promptly signed himself out to see the match.

Unknown to him a group of his friends had arranged to visit him in hospital *en route* to the match, but when they arrived at the ward his bed was empty.

To the amazement of both patients and doctors alike, the six visitors promptly sat round the bed and proceeded to eat all the fruit and drink all the Lucozade they had brought down for their mate.

Scousers of course will go to any length to get into a match.

Legends abound of fans conning their way into Wembley Stadium masquerading as members of the band of the Grenadier Guards, press reporters and even attempting to pass as part of the Royal entourage. Although I'm told that the uttering of 'Oright lad' to a secret service man soon took care of that caper.

European Championships
Bobby Robson and Don Howe have plenty to think about *(left)*; Ruud Gullitt scores for Holland against Russia in the Final *(below)*; and *(bottom)* Ireland's Pat Bonner throws himself at Peter Beardsley's feet to frustrate another scoring chance

One typical piece of Liverpool bravado came in the shape of a delivery boy who worked for a Liverpool bakery. He arrived in London wearing his white baker's coat and carrying a tray of pies which were his passport to some of the most memorable afternoons of his life.

The story goes that a *bona fide* baker's van was turned away on one occasion because the familiar face of the Scouser had already passed the Wembley security men. The biggest gag of all was that there were never any pies on the tray ... only silver foil to protect its imaginary contents.

Reds fans will get up to anything to make their point. I well remember an occasion at Leicester before we were due to play City in an FA Cup replay.

It was a night match, but during the afternoon some Liverpool fans broke into the ground and painted the Filbert Street goal posts red. Officials at the ground made a brave attempt to restore them to their original colour for the match, but the end result was the one and only FA Cup tie settled between pink goal posts!

A million football songs have been conceived and born on the famous Spion Kop terraces. 'Ee-ay-addio' was a children's street game song sung in Liverpool, and adopted of course by the Koppites. The most famous rendition was during my early days at Anfield. We played one match in thick fog at Anfield and a goal was scored at the far end of the pitch from the Kop, prompting the fans to spontaneously inquire 'Who scored the goal... ee-ay-addio... who scored the goal?' Within seconds the supporters at the Anfield Road end struck up 'Hateley scored the goal... ee-ay-addio... Hateley scored the goal.'

Magic stuff.

But if ee-ay-addio must make the Anfield Top Ten there is no doubt that over the years 'You'll Never Walk Alone' has been Top of the Kops. It's been adopted and abused by the supporters of many other clubs, but the only time I recall Liverpool fans singing a variation of their anthem was during a European tie against West German side Cologne when it became 'You'll Never Score Cologne!'

Merseyside humour, of course, abounds in all parts of life... and even death.

It's well known, for instance, that many diehard Liverpool supporters insist on the Kop becoming their last resting place, and there is the story about the Evertonian who attended a solemn farewell to a Liverpudlian friend at the ground. When he returned home his father met him at the door and inquired: 'Did they really scatter the ashes on the Kop then?' 'Yes,' replied the son. 'Scattered to the winds.'

'Well wipe your bloody feet then,' stormed Dad, 'I don't want any Liverpudlian coming into this house.'

Irreverence in Scouse humour is readily accepted by all on Merseyside and if the passion of the game sometimes spills over into the occasional four letter word then that is accepted too.

My old Guv'nor Bill Shankly once dropped his guard live on air while doing a co-commentary alongside Clive Tyldesley of Radio City our local radio station.

The match was a European Cup first round tie between Nottingham Forest and Liverpool at the City ground. Garry Birtles had only been drafted into the Forest team on the previous Saturday and in the opening minutes of his first European tie he scored for Brian Clough's team.

Clive, caught up in the occasion, and ever ready to add a bit of colour to the commentary, screamed at Shanks, 'Well Bill would you believe it ... three days ago we'd never heard of Garry Birtles.'

Shanks picked up his microphone and uttered the immortal reply: 'Well you've f...in' heard of him now.'

Clive was almost speechless, but the interesting thing was, Radio City never received one letter of complaint. As usual the old boy had said precisely what every Liverpool fan was thinking.

Now Shankly became a star on Radio City. He was given his own chat show and it became compulsive listening. Such was the man's status that he could command the biggest names, and on one show the Prime Minister of the day, Sir Harold Wilson, then MP for Huyton, appeared.

Harold, a blarney merchant himself, hardly got a word in edgeways with Shanks, but when finally he was given enough time to crack a tame joke on the subject of football Shanks paused and eyed him across the studio before saying: 'Harold, I think you're trying to steal my thunder.'

Shanks of course was a one off, and his stories are legend. But the truth of the matter is that his successor, Bob Paisley, is a character with a sharp sense of humour too.

His Geordie dialect, as you'll have read elsewhere, isn't always easy to understand – particularly when he adds those strange little words of his own to it. But, believe me, when you can fathom what Bob is saying there are some great one-liners to enjoy.

Like the time Bob signed Israeli international Avi Cohen from Tel Aviv.

Bob was a little perplexed when a visiting Israeli journalist pulled him to one side and asked him if he was aware if Avi was an Orthodox Jew.

'What does that mean?' asked Bob.

'Well,' replied the journalist, 'Avi is bound by the rules of the Jewish faith ... that means he can't play on Saturdays.'

'Don't worry about that,' beamed Bob reassuringly, 'I've got one or two others like that here already!'

On another occasion he was hosting a post-match Anfield press conference when somebody informed him of a double sending-off at Upton Park. West Ham United's big no-nonsense defender Alvin Martin had been dismissed for fighting with Everton's slight and bashful winger Alan Irvine. Bob raised his eyebrows in surprise. 'Sounds like a Duff-Barrett promotion to me,' he concluded.

Ronnie Moran is another evergreen

Ronnie Moran – no-one's really good enough to play for Liverpool!

73

Kenny Dalglish – sharp on and off the field

Anfield personality. He is the sergeant-major of the regime, a man who refuses to believe that Liverpool have got a single player worthy of the red shirt. He sets his standards very high. When the club were linked with the Danish striker Michael Laudrup, his fellow-countryman Jan Molby came into the dressing-room raving about Laudrup's ability and skill. 'You won't believe his ball control, he can do anything with it,' said Molby. 'He can dribble past three men in the space of ten yards, he can pass it fifty yards to a team-mate without even looking, he has tremendous pace and balance, he's an under-rated header of the ball, and of course he scores goals.' Ronnie took a second to weigh up this description of a forward any team in the world would love to have playing for them, then turned to Jan. 'Yes, but can he defend?!' he asked.

The modern Liverpool team has its fair share of jokers, none more practised than the man in charge, Kenny Dalglish. You may recall a postponed FA Cup replay between Liverpool and Luton Town a couple of seasons ago. Anfield was perfectly playable, but heavy snow in the south of England had prevented Luton from reaching Merseyside in time. As usual, the Liverpool players had spent the afternoon of the game asleep in a city-centre hotel, and weren't aware of the postponement until they awoke at about five o'clock. Dalglish and Alan Hansen hatched a plan to keep the news of the cancellation from the young Scottish player Alan Irvine, who had been drafted into the squad as cover. The party had to travel to Anfield by coach to collect their cars in any case, so shortly before leaving the hotel Kenny pulled Irvine to one side and told him he would be making his debut in the match. Because the game had been called off so late in the day there were quite a few fans still milling round the ground when the bus arrived. Irvine had clearly fallen for the stunt, so the manager compounded matters by telling the tall striker that he had decided to try him in midfield. In the dressing-room the players all sat around waiting for the team-talk. The nerves had got to Irvine, who retired to the lavatory to contemplate his big night. When he emerged a couple of minutes later, the dressing-room was empty and all he could hear was the giggling of his team-mates outside in the corridor.

Poor Irvine was the victim of a similar wheeze when he did eventually make his debut in a Testimonial match at Shrewsbury. He was putting Bruce Grobbelaar through his paces during the kick-in when skipper Hansen summoned him to the half-way line to join the pre-match formalities and photographs. There he was, happily posing for the photographers along with the captains, the mascots, the referee and his linesmen, and never bothering to ask why him!

But that sort of thing has always been part and parcel of your Anfield education, and some of the very best Liverpool players have gone through it. Take Steve Nicol for instance... one night he was heading north for an international with Hansen, Dalglish and Graeme Souness. It was freezing cold outside and the snow was belting down, but inside the car the players were warm and Steve was only wearing a T-shirt. As the visibility worsened, Souness pulled over and asked Nicol to jump out and wipe the windscreen. No sooner was he out of the car than it was heading off up the motorway, leaving the poor victim shivering in his T-shirt on the hard shoulder. The next turn-off was several miles away, and it was ten minutes before they returned to collect him.

On another occasion, the senior Scots ganged up on him in the Post House Hotel at Haydock. The team had just sat down to a meal after a Boxing Day game at West Brom because they were at home to Leicester the following afternoon. Steve overheard a conversation in which Souness was asking Dalglish whether his wife was coming over to the hotel to see him. The conversation had, of course, been stage-managed for Nicol, who rushed to the phone to tell his wife to get down to Haydock for this family get-together he was hearing about. By the time he returned to the dinner table, he realised he'd been had. He dashed back to stop his better half, but she had already left.

But the biggest sting that Stevie fell for was out of his respect and affection for Kenny Dalglish. The club's greatest striker had been going through a lean spell in front of goal following his recovery from a fearful cheekbone injury in 1984. His form had been discussed on the terraces and in the pages of the national newspapers, but Liverpool were still picking him, so presumably he was still doing something right. But there was concern, and the stunt was to convince Steve that Kenny had never got over the injury, and spent hours in secret pain, that his health was suffering and his career coming to an end. Arrangements were made for the

Rushie as we know him – wheeling away after scoring!

young defender to visit the great man in his hotel room before a game. The curtains were drawn, the room was quiet, Dalglish was in bed and spoke slowly. Young Steve was clearly upset by the news that his hero was on the wane. He listened to the tale in silence, sad at what he was learning. 'Did you honestly never suspect anything?' asked Dalglish, giving an Oscar-winning performance. 'Not at all,' answered Steve, adding, 'obviously, you've not been playing very well, but I didn't know why!' Touché Kenny!... Oh, and just in case you think his pals were unnecessarily cruel to Steve, rest assured that he is now one of the biggest practical jokers in the squad, and firmly established as its most famous mimic.

No-one escapes the Liverpool wind-ups... even the three-million-pound man Ian Rush.

Rushie got so used to the ploys of Dalglish and company that he almost missed one very important engagement on his very last day with Liverpool ... live on the *Saint and Greavsie Show* on Saturday lunchtime.

Our producer Bob Patience had asked Dalglish to release Rushie for the show as Liverpool were playing Chelsea on the last day of the season ... only twenty minutes from the London Weekend studios.

Kenny did mention it to Ian, but the boyo, well aware that he was bound to be the fall guy in some last day wind-up, reckoned this was it.

Luckily though... for Greavsie and I that is... Ian did sneak off at around 10.30 to phone the studios to ask if he was needed. The answer came back, 'Hell yes... you're on live to the nation in an hour's time.' The

Terry McDermott – always out to impress

panic was on. Ian suddenly had to get from Slough to the South Bank in an hour... no easy matter in London traffic, and it was then the wind-up did start. Kenny and the lads had hidden his shoes, and, after a panic search to no avail, Ian grabbed a pair of Craig Johnstone's Aussie boots and made a mad dash. He limped into the studio with minutes to spare... much to the relief of our backroom staff, who had allocated ten minutes to the Welsh marksman. Mind you there was a happy ending to the day... Ian scored at Stamford Bridge to finish a great Anfield career on a high note.

Terry McDermott was another marvellous jester at the court of Anfield. Alan Kennedy was his most frequent victim. He once got him to phone back a journalist who'd been trying to contact Alan on the players' lounge phone. 'A Mister C. Lion,' said Terry, reading out the number. When Alan got through, it turned out to be the number for Knowsley Safari Park.

But don't let me give you the impression that Liverpool cornered the market in wind-ups and leg-pulls. The Everton team that I did battle with during the sixties was crammed with crazy personalities. Stories abound of Judge Gordon West presiding over Kangaroo Courts, of Roy Vernon smoking in the showers and never getting his cigarette wet, and of Brian Harris taking over as the sales assistant in a city centre shoe-shop after another customer had happened to ask him about the price of some socks.

Harris's favourite trick involved his young son Mark. They lived in Maghull, north of Liverpool, and when he returned home after training Brian would sit six-month-old Mark on the window-sill overlooking the street with the curtain pulled behind him. Then, as people walked past, Brian played the part of a ventriloquist, shouting 'Hello Mrs' to each passing shopper.

But the best Goodison story from the Catterick era features the Scottish full back Sandy Brown, famous on Merseyside for a dramatic headed own goal in a game against Liverpool. Gordon West insists the story has gained in the translation down the years, but others swear that he's just being modest. There was a good deal of publicity at the time about Peter Lorimer's shooting power. Leeds were claiming that Lorimer's shots had been measured at more than seventy miles per hour. Sandy packed a fair wallop himself, and encouraged by Westy and the others became determined to prove that he had a high-velocity shot too. The big goalkeeper vowed to set up a controlled experiment at the club's Bellefield training ground. He would drive alongside the training pitch in his car at seventy miles per hour, and, as he passed a certain point, Sandy would shoot, and the proof would be whether the ball or the car was travelling faster. Versions as to how successful the experiment was do vary, but all agree that gullible Sandy fell for Gordon's plan hook, line and sinker.

In more recent times characters like Andy King, John Bailey and Andy Gray have had Goodison dressing-rooms roaring. Andy's special relationship with the Everton crowd was illustrated by a series of letters he received from a supporter begging Cup Final tickets. He was to believe that the letters were from the fan's solicitors threatening legal action unless a ticket was provided. Their case was based on the fact that the supporter, a large man of forty-nine weighing seventeen stone, had injured himself celebrating Andy's goal against Bayern Munich in the European semi, and was incurring the additional costs of having to buy a stand ticket for Everton games whilst the injury was healing. The Wembley ticket was the suggested settlement.

But the source of the greatest number of Everton stories of recent years is Gordon Lee, the club's manager from 1977 to 1981. Lee was loved by most who met him, and loathed by most of the supporters who didn't. His humour was quite accidental. He had a most simple uncomplicated outlook on the game and indeed life, and was delightfully accident-prone.

Who else could have been caught by the automatic hatches that close over the steps down to the dressing-rooms at the Feyenoord Stadium in Rotterdam?

His collision course with bad luck is well illustrated from his days as manager of Port Vale, a team he guided out of the Fourth Division in 1970 on a shoestring budget. He freely admitted he couldn't afford the quality of players to compete with the best sides even in that Division on level terms, but he did have characters. One afternoon against

mighty Wrexham he fielded two run-through-a-brick-wall strikers of tender years, Sammy Morgan and John James. The Welshmen included the stately Eddie May, a giant of a man in stature and reputation, who scored goals from centre-half as freely as most centre-forwards. Gordon issued instructions to his two young lions to stop May at all costs. They were to shake him up, and if he returned to defence after his first foray forward for a corner with a slight limp and the odd bruise, then Gordon would be the last to complain. Sure enough, when Wrexham were awarded a corner, May started to stride forward imposingly, only to find he had company. Morgan and James had joined him at the half-way line and were bumping and buffeting him even on the way to the box for the corner-kick. When the kick was swung towards May, Morgan jumped in front of him and caught him right between the eyes with the back of his head. The giant was slain, big Eddie was counting sheep in a heap on the edge of the area, but not to be left out James kicked him in the nether regions for luck. Gordon's men had done their job, May had been stopped. Sadly for Port Vale, the referee spotted James's contribution, awarded a penalty, and Wrexham won 1–0!

At Everton his naïve ways left him open to merciless ribbing. On a plane trip home from a pre-season tour to Morocco, he was asked what he had made of Africa, and replied, 'I don't know, I've never been.' He could recall every detail about a player, apart from his name. When he named his young full back Brian Borrows in a squad for the first time, he knew him only by his nickname 'Bugsy', and had to phone down to coach Eric Harrison in order to give his name to the press. He was seen to drink from a finger-bowl, and eating with him was always a perilous occupation because crockery and cutlery were used to illustrate tactical points he was making. So there was always a danger that if you didn't eat your bread roll quickly enough, it would be whipped from your plate to become Bob Latchford in a corner-kick taking place down at Gordon's end of the table.

I hear that Merseyside humour is alive and well at Everton today. When Neville Southall wore a T-shirt bearing the inscription 'I love my wife' at the FA Cup Final a couple of years ago, another of the lads quickly had a T-shirt made up, saying 'I love Nev's wife too!'

Finally, back to Shanks for a fairy-story that sums up the Scouse view of football and their footballing heroes. It's the story of how Bill arrives at the gates of heaven to be met by a worried-looking St Peter. 'Thank goodness you're here, Mr Shankly,' he says. 'Our football team is going through a terrible spell, and we're in desperate need of your expertise and knowledge.' Never one to say no to an invitation to a football match, Shanks journeys over a celestial hill from which he can peer down through the clouds at a football field where a game is in progress. He watches closely for a few minutes then asks St Peter, 'Who is the player wearing the red number seven shirt? He looks like Kenny Dalglish.' St Peter shakes his head and smiles, 'No Bill, that's God.' Shanks is amazed. 'Are you sure, he is so much like Kenny, the way he shields the ball and turns.' 'No,' St Peter assures him, 'that's God.' Bill watches for a few more minutes, but he can see only one player. 'Are you certain that's not Kenny Dalglish? Watch how he brings the others into the game, then tries to curl the ball past the keeper on the turn, it's Kenny all over.' 'No,' says St Peter once again. 'That is God. He just THINKS he's Kenny Dalglish!'

7 A DROP OF SCOTCH

As someone who is supposed to be the modern-day hammer of the Scots, can I say that whoever described the mob north of Hadrian's Wall as dour needed his head looked at.

While I am prone to giving the old Jocks a bit of a poke every now and then on the *Saint and Greavsie Show* I have to admit that over the years they have given me more laughs and better stories than any other race.

My old mates at Tottenham, Dave Mackay, Alan Gilzean and the late great John White, at times had me in stitches, and some of their capers are well recorded in the first edition of this book.

And even now when I go north of the border I'm treated like a long lost friend and regaled with tales of the unexpected ... most of them hilarious.

In this chapter I must admit I've had a bit of help from some mates north of the border ... but with characters such as those I'm writing about you can be sure that smiles are the order of the day.

For the one thing the Scots can do is laugh at themselves. I remember Russ Abbott, that funny, funny man, talking about launching his Jimmy McJimmy character ... the loon with the red hair and the kilt and braces. Russ was a bit worried the Scots might take umbrage ... but in fact they've loved every minute of it ... and why not? A laugh at oneself makes sure the ego stays normal size.

I start off with a man I've the utmost respect for ... big Billy McNeill, who, after a tough time in England with Manchester City and Aston Villa, returned to Parkhead in triumph last season and won the League and Cup double for Celtic.

It was a tremendous achievement for the Big Man particularly since it was Celtic's Centenary Year. But I wasn't surprised. I played against Billy often enough to know that he oozes class, and despite what some of

the media hatchet men said you don't lose ability and that special type of leadership McNeill has overnight.

Throughout all the downs Billy kept his dignity... and his sense of humour... and for story-telling there's few better. Take this one about the first time he was in charge at Parkhead.

Celtic had suffered a rare mid-week defeat, and when Caesar got to the ground next morning he was out to bury someone not praise him.

Says Billy: 'I was in a filthy mood when I arrived and when I saw four players in the treatment room with their feet in ice buckets, I thought they were skiving. I ordered them through to the dressing-room for my post-mortem and just to let them know I meant business I volleyed one of the buckets in behind them and then stormed into the dressing-room after them.

'I'd forgotten though that the ice had scattered everywhere and I went skidding all over the place before landing on my backside on the floor. I got up and dared any of the players to laugh then got the hell out as quickly as possible.

'The inevitable happened. As soon as the door closed behind me the place erupted with laughter... with one Charlie Nicholas leading the hilarity.'

Billy of course was also a big success at Aberdeen before joining Celtic as manager for the first time, and one player he had there was Ian Fleming – a hard-hitting striker whom he relied on to put himself about a bit when it mattered. But McNeill remembers one game when Fleming got it all wrong and nearly got sent off for his trouble.

'We were playing Rangers, who had Stewart Kennedy in goal, and I told Ian... let him know you're there very early on. "No problem boss," said Ian. "Anyway the referee, Hugh

Above: Celtic's Big Two – captain Roy Aitken and manager Billy McNeill with the Championship trophy – before Big Billy's blazer took a dunking!

Opposite: Celtic skipper Roy Aitken, as involved as ever, clashes with Dundee United's Flying Finn, Mixu Paatelainen, in the 1988 Scottish Cup final. Celtic won 2–1 to clinch the double

Alexander, is a pal of mine from Kilmarnock... he'll let me away with murder."

'The game had only gone a few minutes when Kennedy gathered a long throw-in. In went Flem with all the finesse of a Panzer tank... and late with it. That's when the Old Pals act came in... Fleming was promptly booked by his mate and told "any more like that and you're off."'

Any readers may remember the scenes on *Saint and Greavsie* when McNeill and his assistant manager Tommy Craig were dumped in the Parkhead bath after clinching the league title last April. Billy accepted the dunking and settled down good suit and all with a bottle of champers ... and well deserved too.

But one of Scottish soccer's best kept

secrets came after the Cup Final win over Dundee United which gave Celtic the double... how the winning manager walked right into double trouble.

Now Billy reckons himself to be fairly streetwise in the ways of high-spirited footballers... after all he's been amongst them for almost thirty years.

But the post-final celebrations climaxed for the big fella when the Celtic masseur Jimmy Steel, a great character, slipped up to Billy and told him quietly the players would like a quick word. The unsuspecting McNeill walked straight into a barrage of profiteroles and chocolate cake... yet another suit was on its way to the cleaners!

Over the years of course there have been many great characters amongst the managers in Scottish football, and surely one of the biggest was genial pipe-smoking Jerry Kerr, the man who originally took Dundee United out of the wilderness and into the First Division. Tales of Jerry are legend.

Now Jerry was one of the old school. A former Rangers attacker he never claimed to be an Einstein, and when soccer became a numbers game he gathered his players around him one day and said 'Now lads... listen up... we're going to play a 4-3-3 today.'

To which keeper Thomson Allan replied, 'Am I not getting a game then boss?'

Arrangements weren't Jerry's strong suit either. He once left his players to make their own preparations for a month-long world tour. One player, Tommy O'Hara, turned up with a brown paper parcel under his arm containing one shirt, a toothbrush and his shaving gear ... that was his lot for the entire trip.

On the same trip – in Mexico – Jerry also failed to grasp the intricacies of drinking Tequila. Now everyone knows that the Mexican hooch should be taken with a pinch of salt... and Jerry did take his pinch. The only problem was he snuffed it instead of tasting it before swallowing the Tequila – leaving himself gasping for breath and his players howling with laughter.

Jerry I'm told did it again at the end of the tour... this time in Athens, when he asked a hotel receptionist: 'How many draculas to the pound?'

In his time at Tannadice Jerry did a wonderful job with United, and it's worth remembering that he guided them to a double European win over Barcelona in the sixties... a feat United under Jim McLean repeated only two seasons ago in that great UEFA Cup run.

Jerry knew his football all right, but on one occasion he had his players scratching their heads with a baffling team choice. United's star striker Alan Gordon had been ruled out of a vital game with a groin injury and then on match day Morris Stevenson, a possible deputy, complained of chest pains and was found to have two cracked ribs.

It was in the days when only one substitute was allowed in Scottish football and, with the reserves already off to Kilmarnock, Jerry's team choice was getting rather limited. To Alan Gordon's astonishment he was told he would play, while an injury-free Denis Gillespie would be on the bench.

'Why's that?' enquired Gordon. 'Because I need a fit sub on the bench,' answered Jerry.

Once when Jerry dropped another attacker, Tony Dunne, the player angrily demanded an explanation. 'Why me? A lot of other players in the side are rubbish,' complained Tony. To which Jerry replied: 'Listen son – I'll pick the rubbish here.'

Another great Scottish character was little Willie Ormond, the man who guided Scotland to the World Cup Finals in 1974. Willie

Wee Willie Ormond and Scotland trainer
Roddy McKenzie. Willie was only a goal away
from glory in West Germany

was the left-winger in Hibs' Famous Five
forward line of the fifties which consisted of
Gordon Smith, Bobby Johnstone, Lawrie
Reilly, Eddie Turnbull and Ormond... what a
magical front line that was.

And Wee Willie did a marvellous job for
Scotland. I'll never forget that World Cup
side in 1974 so nearly putting Brazil, the
favourites, out in the first round of matches.
I was out of my seat by the telly trying to
guide one shot by Billy Bremner from close
range past the keeper. Sadly, although the
Scots returned from the tournament as the
only country not to have lost a game... they

scored one win and two draws against Zaire,
Brazil and Yugoslavia... they went out of
the tournament on goal difference.

Ormond knew players... and he was a
marvellous man. Any time he was in
company he had a ready smile and a story...
and some of his stories could easily be
classed as 'tales of the unexpected'.

Like the time he took St. Johnstone, a
small provincial club, into the UEFA Cup
and drew mighty Hamburg, then carrying
all before them in West Germany, with Uwe
Seeler, that great German striker, their main
man. The tale is told that after gaining a
highly creditable 1–1 draw in the Volkspark
Stadium, the Saints players went off to
celebrate in Hamburg's notorious red light
district of St Paulis. As the revelry got out of
hand there was a fracas in a nightclub and
next morning, as the players boarded the
plane for home, Willie cast a rueful eye over
his motley crew, bumps, bruises and black
eyes all too apparent, and murmured drily:
'Aye! Yer all learning about this European
football right enough.'

Lovely!

Then there was the time Willie, much
against his better judgement, was persuaded
to go fishing by his assistant manager at St
Johnstone Frank Christie.

The pair went to the River Tay near
Muirton Park, Perth. Willie told me: 'Frank
had no luck, the rain never stopped pouring
and I got rapidly bored. I was standing on
the bank, sheltering under trees, when I saw
a salmon swimming through the shallows.

'I jumped into the water and toe-ended it
on to the bank with my left peg. I'd scored a
fair few goals with it, but this was the first
time it had got me a fish. I didn't know
whether to write to Rothmans or the *Guin-
ness Book of Records*.

'You can imagine the stick Big Frank took.

Another near miss for Scotland against Brazil in 1974 – Joe Jordan as usual gives the opposing defence plenty to think about

I'd caught a salmon at my first attempt with an old boot and he, the expert, had failed with all his fancy gear. But he cheered up when I sold the fish to a local hotel and we had a right good bevvy.'

You know I do a bit of salmon fishing myself on the Tay... but I've never thought of kicking the brutes onto the bank. Next time I'll leave my rod at home and get the old boots off the peg!

Very few people knew that Willie was a veteran of the Arctic Convoys... he kept that fact to himself. But prior to the start of the 1974 World Cup in West Germany, Willie knew fear like he'd never known on those dangerous journeys to Russia.

That was when Celtic winger Jimmy Johnstone decided to go boating on the River Clyde in the middle of the night after leaving Scotland's team headquarters.

Willie, who by this time had become Scotland's international manager, later confessed: 'When I saw Wee Jinky disappearing over the horizon in a dinghy, I thought: What'll Big Jock (Stein) say if he's drooned?' Thankfully, Wee Jimmy was rescued and Willie's worst fears weren't realised.

Football missed Willie Ormond when he passed on a few years ago. He was a fine man who deserved all the success he got...

and his humour will never be forgotten.

If Willie was a funny man the same could not be said of the man who played inside forward to him both in that great Hibs team and for Scotland – Eddie Turnbull.

Now I've never had many dealings with Eddie, or Ned as he was known in Scotland, but a journalist once told me, 'Finding humour in Ned Turnbull is like finding a virgin in a maternity ward.' Very nice!

Ned, I'm told from my spies north of the border, was as feared as a manager at Aberdeen and Hibs as he was as an iron-hard player at Easter Road.

Yet he has been credited with one of the best one-liners of all time when he gave a dressing down one day to the aforementioned Alan Gordon, who eventually moved from Dundee United to Hearts to Hibs.

Alan, who now does an excellent job as a football expert with Radio Forth in Edinburgh, was a clever lad and a qualified accountant as well as a footballer and he shook with laughter as Ned raged at him, 'You know the trouble with you ... all your brains are in your head.' Brilliant that!

He was also slightly off-target when he instructed one of his Aberdeen players to 'get the ball over that full head's back!'

In my day, of course, Rangers were the dominant side in Scotland. Scot Symon was their manager and I well remember two marvellous ties we had with the Ibrox Club during our European Cup Winners Cup winning run in 1963.

Rangers had some marvellous players – Eric Caldow, Jim Baxter, Davie Wilson, Jimmy Millar, Ralph Brand to mention but a few. We beat them home and away in the end but not without a struggle in two of the greatest matches I ever played in ... from memory it was 3–2 at Ibrox and 5–2 at White Hart Lane.

Now Scot Symon was not a man known for his humour, but he did tell me one very funny story from the days of his predecessor Bill Struth.

Struth ruled Ibrox with an iron hand ... so much so that the players were frightened to ask for a pay rise ... and that included their skipper Jock Shaw, whom the boys had wanted to be their spokesman. But their great international inside forward Torry Gillick was a cheeky so-and-so and he was persuaded to state the lads' case.

Struth, unused to any player appearing at his door, boomed at Gillick: 'What are you doing here, what do you want?'

To which Gillick replied: 'Me and nine others want a pay rise. Jock Shaw doesn't.' Needless to say none of them got one. And Gillick was transferred South soon after!

Rangers were involved in a border drama when they were returning by coach through Checkpoint Charlie after a UEFA Cup tie against Dinamo Dresden.

International centre half Ron McKinnon had a pocketful of East German marks left. These, he was told by his team-mates, were of no use in the West.

When the coach stopped in no man's land to be checked out by armed guards, Big Ron exited from a rear door – intent on returning to the nearest shop to spend the cash.

His rash move caused a furore and brought a stern rebuke from Manager Scot Symon.

When Celtic were the toast of Europe, their manager Jock Stein was less than pleased when he caught several of his players in a late-night drinking session in an hotel room.

In an angry and dramatic gesture, Big Jock grabbed a bottle of vodka and hurled it into a bath.

But, despite the Big Man's efforts, the bottle refused to break, the anger subsided, and the players escaped a real rollicking.

Humour still abounds in Scottish dressing-rooms though, and only a year ago Ian Porterfield, while manager of Aberdeen, found himself putting his foot in it before his players at Pittodrie.

Ian had just signed Charlie Nicholas from Arsenal and was trying to make it clear Charlie was just another team member and should be treated as such.

'After all he's only got two arms and two legs like everyone else,' he said.

'Not much for half a million quid,' flashed back the quip from the assembled players.

As I've often said Jim Baxter was one of my favourite all-time players. Slim Jim loved the big stage, and on one or two occasions he made we English suffer at Wembley... I'm thinking of 1963 and 1967 in particular.

And Jim, as Saint has said, was a real character. Maybe Jim took a little too long to come down to England – I don't know – but having watched him at his peak I reckon he would have been rated amongst the greats in the game had he starred for the likes of Spurs, Arsenal or Manchester United.

Jim, of course, joined Rangers from Raith Rovers, the little team from Kirkcaldy in Fife, and he tells a lovely tale about Bert Herdman, who ran that club as his own for years.

Bert, it appears, was another old boss who never quite got to grips with modern-day tactics and Jim tells the story of how he would say to his players, 'Kick the ball in the air whenever you get the chance ... the opposition can't intercept it up there.'

Now there's logic for you!

Jock Stein, of course, had a million stories, but he used to be particularly tickled by the endeavours of Tam Ferguson, the supremo who held Stirling Albion together for years

at the other Annfield.

Jock used to tell the story of how Celtic visited Annfield in a Cup tie and after the game Old Tam – a real rough diamond – was holding court as usual in the Big House... a rambling grey sandstone building used for an after-match tipple.

The Celtic board consisted of several big businessmen and they were led by Sir Robert Kelly, one of the straightest men in football and one of the most prim and proper.

Stein admits to spluttering his tea over the room when, in full earshot of the Celtic board and their ladies, someone asked Tam if he was happy with the draw Albion had achieved that night.

'Happy?' quoth Old Tam, 'I'm as happy as shit!'

Even Big Jock was frightened to look at Sir Robert's face!

Ferguson left a legacy of stories when he died. He always ran Albion on a shoestring and the story is told how a young player – Martin Valentine - tackled him about his wages being short.

Old Tam snorted: 'There's nae money. Take these two pheasants and half a dozen eggs instead.'

Compliments of that left peg of Willie Ormond no doubt!

An opinionated man, Tam was apparently never afraid to express himself ... often taking the fans' side against his own players.

Once when a fan criticised a player for failing to tackle, Ferguson shot out of his seat and roared: 'Tackle? That yin could nae tackle an auld woman on a lonely road.'

All lovely stories, and all of which emphasise my original argument that the Scots have a great sense of humour. I know that at first hand... the Saint has to sit beside me every Saturday lunchtime!

8 MANAGERS AND PLAYERS

Football management can be a hard life ... but it can also be a hilarious one. In this chapter some of our mates in the game – big names such as Ron Atkinson, Alex Ferguson, Bobby Campbell, George Graham, Frank McLintock and Billy McNeill – share their funny moments ... both as managers and players.

Like Greavsie I'm a big fan of Ron Atkinson. I felt he got a raw deal at Manchester United in the end. After all he had guided them to two Cup Final successes and had always attempted to put an entertaining, personality-packed side onto the Old Trafford pitch. He was also, let it be noted, up against some great Merseyside sides in the Liverpool and Everton teams he competed against as United boss.

And Atko has never lost his sense of humour. He has a gag for every occasion and loves re-telling the stories which he has accumulated over the years ... all well worth hearing.

Like the 'Peter Barnes team-talk'. Now any manager will tell you the worst thing you can do in a pre-match team-talk is to make a mistake. Players will pounce on it, and like elephants they never forget ... and that is why Atko will never live down one such occasion which became legendary

Ron Atkinson – a great story teller, and not a bad manager either!

90

during his first spell at West Bromwich Albion.

The Baggies were playing at Arsenal and because of a traffic problem warning Atko pulled the pre-match team-talk at the hotel forward from one o'clock to noon.

As usual Big Ron was thorough. He went through the defensive and midfield commitments before concentrating on the role to be played by Peter Barnes, the England winger he had signed from Manchester City for £600,000.

'Barnsey will be our key man. I want you to be making runs along both wings, you've to take the penalties, free kicks and throw-ins and I want to see perpetual motion.'

For fifteen minutes Atko extolled the virtues of Barnsey and how he would be the man to win the match for the team.

Then, just as he was about to ram home his final point on the subject, he looked slowly around the team group and realised to his horror, that 'Barnsey' wasn't there. He had forgotten the changed time of the team meeting!

'Don't worry boss,' grinned Gary Owen, 'Barnsey never listens anyway!'

Fans often ask if managers treat their great players differently from the others. The diplomatic answer is 'Certainly not'. The truth is 'Definitely yes'.

It happened to Atko with one of the biggest of all players while on an Australian tour with Manchester United.

His captain Bryan Robson did not turn up for lunch with the team and no explanation was offered. Big Ron was raging and Robbo was ordered to Atko's room for a dressing down. Four hours and six bottles of champagne later they both missed dinner....

Big Ron also tells of the day my old guv'nor came up with a gem... typical Shanks.

'During my first spell as manager at West Brom I used to invite Shanks to join our squad on match days. He had been pensioned off by Liverpool and just having him around the Albion set-up was a great bonus for us.

'His presence was enough of a gee-up and his wit was fabulous.

'Shanks was having lunch with a few players before we played Nottingham Forest in a Cup tie, and Willie Johnston, that great little Scottish winger, commented that while most clubs seemed to be cutting their playing staffs, he had read that Newcastle United still had fifty-four professionals.

'"Aye son," said Shanks. "None of them can play... but it's easing the unemployment situation on Tyneside!"'

Atko also tells plenty of stories against himself, and one of them came following United's win over Everton in the 1985 FA Cup Final.

The victorious United squad arrived back after the match at the Royal Lancaster Hotel and much champagne flowed.

By the time Jimmy Hill and a television outside broadcast unit arrived for a live insert into the *Match of the Day* programme, the bubbly had gone down rather well – particularly with Big Ron.

Jimmy had lined up goalscorer Norman Whiteside and Atko for interviews, but by the time Ron's turn came the champagne was taking its revenge.

As the cameras whirred Ron was a slurring, grunting, gesticulating mess. Wisely he decided to shut up. It was then Hilly chipped in: 'That's the first time I've ever seen you speechless, Ron.' Whiteside, quick as a flash was in: 'He's not speechless Jimmy – he's legless!'

Atko is one of life's jokers and he once pulled a real fast one on the well-respected sports journalist Neil Harman, now a tennis

writer with the *Daily Mail*, but then an ambitious young football reporter with the *Birmingham Evening Mail*. It was in the days when Ron was looking for a replacement for Laurie Cunningham, whom he had just sold from West Brom to Real Madrid for a million pounds.

It was well known in football circles that Atko was looking for an international striker to replace the Black Flash, as Cunningham was known at the time.

As a joke Sammy Morgan, the Irish international striker who had played with Ron at Cambridge United, phoned him to say that he was an international striker playing with Sparta Rotterdam and was available. Sammy was near the end of his career and it was all a laugh amongst friends, but Atko mentioned to Neil Harman that he had had a phone call from an international striker, but was sworn to secrecy as to who it was. Harman persisted and Atko realising a wind-up was on, said, 'OK. You've got the story but you must sit on it until tomorrow. I tell you one thing it's not Neeskens or Cruyff, but he is rated one of the best young players in Holland.'

'I need a name,' pleaded Neil.

'Rudi Wakening,' countered Atko with a straight face. 'He doesn't play for one of the fashionable clubs. He's with A.Z. and they signed him from a third division side called Vastas Leep last season.'

Neil, happy with his scoop, went back to the office and, being the good journalist he is, searched the record books. Naturally none showed any sign of Rudi Wakening.

And Neil phoned Atko the next morning to admit his rude awakening had come in the middle of the night... when he woke up with

Norman Whiteside celebrates his Cup-winning goal with Kevin Moran. Later Norman was to stitch up Big Ron

a start and realised he had been stitched up like a kipper.

Atko over the past few years has been a great tourist with the ITV Sport football team... and many a laugh we've had too.

One magic moment we still laugh about came in the final of the 1980 European Championship match between West Germany and Belgium. Ron was co-commentator in the match with Brian Moore. At half-time Mooro, impressed with Bernd Schuster's first-half performance, commented during a commercial break how much he reminded him of a young Alan Hudson in his days at Chelsea. Ron promptly offered Brian what he felt a better comparison. 'Schuster is German, blond, dominates midfield – he's an absolute ringer for Gunther Netzer, the star of that great West German team of the same championships in 1972.'

Mooro agreed and made a note to use it in his commentary. As the second half began, the ball was with Schuster and the commentary went something like this:

Moore: 'Now it's Schuster for West Germany and I must say Ron Atkinson... how much he must remind you of the great Gunther Netzer from the German team of 1972.'

Atkinson: 'That's a fair point, Brian, but I must say he reminds me more of the young Alan Hudson when he played for Chelsea.'

For the next minute there was no commentary. The whole production team, including the two commentators, were speechless with laughter.

Another Atko wind-up took place in, of all places, China, when West Brom became the first English football team to visit there in 1978.

It was the trip when Albion midfielder John Trewick became famous when asked what he thought of the Great Wall of China.

Karl Heinz Rummenigge (West Germany) in action in the 1980 European Championship final against Belgium

He answered, 'When you've seen one wall you've seen them all!'

What was never reported back was how John, who went on to play for Newcastle, Oxford and Birmingham, became the victim of the Great Chinese Wind-Up.

West Brom were to play the Chinese national team in their first game and it was regarded as the biggest sporting event in the country for years. John had been injured and couldn't play, but Atko told him that to make up for his disappointment he would be allowed to carry the Union Jack at the front of the team when they marched onto the pitch.

John wasn't exactly taken by the idea, but

Atko had gone to work. He had briefed everyone in the party to persuade John to do it... telling him that to carry the flag was the biggest honour any sportsman could have in China. Everyone was in on the act. Reporters covering the trip did mock interviews with John and even the British Ambassador played the game when he singled him out at an Embassy garden party and congratulated him on 'his honour'. By now John had swallowed the bait hook, line and sinker and had even relayed the news to his family by phone.

The charade was kept hot for four days and then John's big moment came. Atko even told him how to hold the Union Jack... with a slightly crooked arm. He was to bring the flag to attention on the first note of our National Anthem.

As West Brom marched onto the field before 80,000 Chinese spectators, John was at the front of a West Brom team almost doubled up. At the first note, the arm straightened and the flag was brought smartly to attention. Eleven Albion players, two substitutes, the assistant manager and manager all had tears in their eyes and so, I expect, did the British Ambassador... tears of laughter at the unsuspecting Trewick.

John didn't realise it all had been a wind-up until later... when everyone from Ambassador down were all treated to a barrage of vintage Geordie language.

Atko even has an amusing tale to tell about one of the most sensational stories in British World Cup history... the sending home of Scotland's Willie Johnston following his taking of a banned pill during the 1978 World Cup finals in Argentina.

Atko was wee Willie's manager at West Brom and was on hand to guard him from the world press when he landed at Heathrow.

Ron was aware that Willie, a prankster himself, might burst out laughing as he left the aircraft and warned him, 'Don't laugh Willie – you're in disgrace.'

Willie chirped, 'Look on the bright side boss. We should get a great sponsorship... from Boots... next season.'

Stifling a smile, and wanting to give Willie a quick chance to explain that it was medication and not hard drugs that had produced a negative test result, Ron agreed to a *Grandstand* interview, and Bob Wilson was sent to escort the two from the airport to London. Heathrow officials showed Atko, Willie and Bob a private route from the airport to escape the hordes of pressmen.

Atko takes up the story: 'We took off in my car and I bombed it up the M4 to London. I was driving a big fast Jaguar and had got caught up in the excitement of the chase and the drama. Looking in the mirror I saw two sets of motorcycle headlights... we were being followed.

'In best movie tradition I turned sharply off the motorway at Chiswick and zigzagged my way through the maze of small streets... still the headlights were there.

'It became a bit like *Starsky and Hutch*. I did a U-turn and drove up a one-way street. I stopped at a green light and then sped off as it went red. I even reversed into the two motorcyclists, but nothing would shake them off.

'Finally we reached the TV studios at Shepherd's Bush and as the barrier was lifted sure enough in behind us roared the two motorcyclists. There was no escape.

'As I pulled up they roared across, then to my amazement saluted us. It turned out they were BBC outriders sent to protect us – in case we were followed!'

One of my great friends in football is Frank McLintock, a great centre half who I had the privilege of playing alongside for

Scotland. Frank, of course, was captain of the great Arsenal double-winning side in the seventies, and only last season, as assistant manager of Millwall, he helped John Docherty guide the London club into the First Division for the first time in history.

Frank is also a collector and teller of great football stories, and his experiences both as manager and player have been, at times, hilarious.

In his early playing days he was with Leicester City, a club he was later to manage, and he tells of his City days alongside Billy Hodgson, who was a real Norman Wisdom lookalike. And Billy, a fantastic little player, had the reputation of being just as funny as his double... even though at times it was unintentional.

On one occasion City were due to play Sheffield Wednesday and Matt Gillies was presiding over the usual pre-match team talk.

Now Wednesday had a good striker called Tommy McAnerny, and Matt, after telling Big Frank to pick up the winger at corner kicks, turned to little Billy and said 'Billy you must pick up Tommy McAnerny.' Billy immediately protested, 'But boss that's not fair.'

Gillies, puzzled at the outburst, asked why, and almost collapsed as Billy said, 'Because Frank's only picking up one player... I've got three... Tommy, Mac and Ernie!'

Needless to say the team talk that followed was lost in the howls of laughter that accompanied it.

Frank, like Atko, also tells a good story against himself and one which happened early in his career is a good 'un.

Youngsters are always keen to learn and Frank was no exception. Before one important game he noticed the trainer put a spoon-ful of salt into eleven cups of water and told the team to drink up. Frank, inquisitive as ever, asked the reason for the salt and was told, 'It will enable you to run further over the ninety minutes.'

Frank says: 'Being young and green I didn't know the salt was really to prevent dehydration. I just thought, well, if one spoonful does that... just imagine how far I could run with a jugful inside me.

'When the players left the dressing-room, I hung back, piled salt into a jugful of water, and drank the lot!

'You can imagine the effect. I soon had a thirst like Oliver Reed on a good day.

'I somehow managed to get through the first half, but when the half-time whistle sounded I was off up the tunnel like a rocket looking for relief.

'The rest of the lads had an orange or a cup of tea. Not me – I settled for six jugs of water. In fact if the groundsman had filled the bath early I'd have drunk that as well!

'Then came the second half. I played the last forty-five minutes feeling like a water bed on legs. The final whistle just couldn't come too soon... and again I was off like a jet... this time in search of some more relief... in the loo.

'When I came out the lads were already having their bath and I dived straight in, hoping it would make me feel better. They still wonder why I spent the next ten minutes floating on the top of the water!'

Another of Frank's stories concerns the Irish player Liam Brady.

'Towards the end of my career at Arsenal I had the pleasure of playing with Liam "Chippy" Brady, the immensely talented young Irishman who has since starred with Juventus and West Ham.

'Liam was obviously one for the future, but like all kids was a bit green... and on one memorable occasion he had the rest of us creased with laughter.

'It happened during a match against Everton. Chippy got something in his eye, and our trainer Fred Street was called on to have a look.

'Chippy was holding his face in agony and Fred asked what happened. Liam replied, "There was a scramble in the goalmouth and something went in my eye."

'Fred, becoming more concerned, asked "Which one?" Brady replied, "The North Bank end." Fred, becoming desperate, as in those days there were no substitutes, shouted "I meant which eye?"

'Anyway he stuck a sponge on the eye and Chippy played on. A few minutes later he was over at Fred again. Fred immediately poured out some Optrex into an eyebath and said, "Here make it quick." Liam, thinking Fred had said "Take it quick" raised the eye bath to his lips and, before Fred could stop him, had swallowed the lot.

'Fred was astounded, but Chippy just pulled a face saying "This stuff's foul." Then touching his eye he added "And it doesn't work either. I can still feel it."'

Greavsie

Another of Frank's Irish tales concerns his old mate Terry Mancini, who was getting on a bit when he joined up at Arsenal, but looked even older because he was bald.

When he first arrived at Highbury it was reported that a director saw him and commented to Bertie Mee 'But he's got no hair.' To which Bertie replied: 'What do you want him to do... play football or race greyhounds?'

The director got an even bigger surprise when Terry was chosen to play for the Republic of Ireland... and it was a surprise for Big Frank too, who says, 'Now how can anyone with a name like Mancini be considered Irish. I mean the Irish do go to some lengths in order to get a player. Terry used to kid us that he got his qualifications through a second cousin twice removed whose auntie had an affair with an Irish deck hand on the midnight crossing from Liverpool to Dublin.

'Anyway, Terry turned out for the Republic against Poland. As usual the two teams lined up for the anthems. It was all new to Terry, who was a bit overawed by it

Frank McLintock, Arsenal's 'Double' skipper – a man with a million stories

97

all standing beside Don Givens.

'As the band struck up the first anthem the TV cameras started to go along the line of the team. By the time they got to the end the band was still playing and the director went back along the line. By this time the band seemed to Terry to be playing the fifteenth chorus and he turned to Don Givens and commented, "I don't know how these Poles can put up with this before every game." To which Don replied, "You'd better get used to it... this one's ours!"'

One of Frank's great mates is George Graham, now guiding Arsenal back to their rightful place amongst the élite of English football, and of course a fellow member of the double-winning side.

George, another Scot, has done a wonderful job at Highbury packing his team with some of the best young talent in Britain and already it has brought rich rewards... two Littlewoods Cup final appearances on the trot... winning the first against Liverpool and losing 3–2 in the second to Luton in one of the most dramatic and entertaining finals ever to be seen at Wembley.

George as a player was as smart as his gear. Known as Gentleman George, his skills as an inside forward took him not only to Highbury but to Manchester United under Tommy Docherty, who had first spotted his talent as a youngster.

Now he's one of Britain's top bosses... known as a disciplinarian but ready to smile at some of the funny moments he's had both as manager and player.

Interestingly enough, it was an injury to Frank McLintock which set George on his way as one of the best inside forwards in British football. George had been a recognised centre forward with both Villa and Chelsea before signing for Arsenal as a striker. At that time Big Frank played wing,

Top: George Graham of Arsenal – a strict disciplinarian but loves the funny side of the game

Above: 'Uncle' Joe Mercer – one of football's most loved characters, but he wasn't always smiling!

half for the Gunners. One day when Frank was injured George was asked to play in midfield. He stepped in and had a blinder. The team won 5–2, but George was dropped! But the die was cast – a class inside forward had been born.

George's first boss was the great Joe Mercer... Joe took George south from Scotland as a fifteen-year-old to Villa Park... and George has a secret to tell about old Joe, who is looked upon as one of football's most benign figures.

'As a lad I used to watch Joe when the team would come in at half-time or full-time losing or beaten. The first thing Joe went for was the laundry skip... he used to give it one helluva kick.

'It became a joke whenever anyone asked what it was like to work under Joe... we used to say "He kicks a lovely skip!"'

It was Tommy Docherty who really spotted George's potential. The Graham talent intrigued the Doc, so much so that he 'signed' him three times... for Chelsea, Manchester United and Scotland.

Says George: 'The Doc was a big influence. He took chances, and being a spotter of good players the chances usually paid off.

'I remember when he was manager of Scotland he took what many considered a scratch team out to South America to play in a mini world cup tournament. In fact we played three, drew two and lost only one, 1–0 to Brazil, before almost 200,000 soccer crazy Brazilians in the Maracana.'

George remembers how the Doc once got rid of the Eusebio menace when Scotland played Portugal.

'It was my debut match for Scotland and the pre-match tactics talk at Largs was hilarious. Doc got out a basket of fruit. Every Portuguese player was nominated by a banana, apple or pear, but there was only one fruit for Eusebio... a black grape. I'd heard of him being called the Black Pearl before but never the Black Grape.

'As we stifled laughs the Doc went through each Portuguese player, pushing aside each fruit. But when he came to Eusebio he said, "There's only one thing to do with this fellow... eat him up." With that he popped the black grape in his mouth... to the roars of the Scottish team.

'Mind you, it worked. We did beat Portugal that night and Eusebio hardly kicked a ball.'

George's days under Tommy Doc at Chelsea also stir the memories ... for it brought him into contact with his great mate Terry Venables for the first time. Now they are Arsenal and Tottenham managers, respectively, both looking forward to the great London derbies between their clubs... and George knows that he'll have to have his thinking cap on when he meets T.V.'s men.

He says: 'Even in those days Terry was a great thinker of the game. We had some marvellous players in that Chelsea side... people like Johnny Hollins, Terry, Bobby Tambling, Peter Bonetti and latterly Peter Osgood.

'But Terry always knew best. He used to rehearse the free-kicks with us all in a corner of the pitch while Doc was away doing something else.

'We would come off the pitch having won a match with three goals from three different free-kick situations and Doc would say "That was marvellous lads... bloody marvellous." Terry used to just look over and give that famous wink.'

Doc might have been the boss off the pitch... Terry was certainly the guv'nor on it. And Venables was not the only joker in the Chelsea pack... Johnny Hollins loved a laugh too. One day when the pair got together for a piece of nonsense some holidaymakers got it in the neck.

Explains George: 'We were on a trip and were delayed at Heathrow for some reason.

'Terry and Johnny spotted an empty desk and decided a wind-up was on. Somehow they managed to nick some airport stewards' caps and jackets and as a group of holiday-makers gathered they shouted "Over here!" The lads looking on were helpless as Terry and Johnny put the poor passengers through the mill, looking at their tickets and causing untold chaos. It was only when some official ground staff appeared TV and Holly disappeared... leaving some very irate holiday-makers behind.'

As I've said, George, like Frank McLintock, was part of the great Arsenal double-winning team, and was credited with the equaliser against Liverpool in the 1971 FA Cup Final... that is until a hawk-eyed Brian Moore noticed on a replay a touch from Eddie Kelly just after George made contact.

So was it Graham or Kelly who got the equaliser? Says George: 'It's history now but I might tell the true story in my memoirs. At the end of the day Charlie George got the winner and both Eddie and I finished up with Cup Winners' medals and as part of Arsenal folklore.

'But we had a joke in the dressing-room. The reason I got credited was that all the lads ran to kiss me when the ball went in the net... not because I had scored but to avoid kissing Eddie.

'You see in those days Eddie had very heavy acne and the lads all told me "There's no way we're kissing that bugger!"'

George is known as a disciplinarian at Highbury, and a fellow Scot, Alex Ferguson, has the same reputation at Old Trafford.

Fergie, though, has always seen the funny side of football and never more so than at Aberdeen, where he kept a firm hand but did encourage his staff to enjoy a joke.

And for one set of young players at Pittodrie the joke was on them after a 'boys'

Terry Venables and Diego Maradona *(above)* in the Football League v Rest of the World Centenary match – two of football's great tricksters. *Left:* Manchester United manager, Alex Ferguson. Fergie's serious here, but he loves a joke

fun' night at their Aberdeen digs. Alex was called late one night by the landlady, who looked after several of the club's young players. She was complaining bitterly about a storage heater being broken and Fergie tried to reason with her that boys will be boys and at eighteen years old some horse play was inevitable from time to time.

The woman retorted, 'It wasn't horses they were playing... it was hide and seek!'

Fergie, dumbstruck, blurted: 'But eighteen-year-olds don't play hide and seek.'

'Your lot do!' came the reply.

A dressing down was in order and the next morning before they had time to confer they were wheeled in one by one to explain. The first four denied all knowledge, even showing indignation that anyone should think they would play hide and seek. But after a grilling the fifth bloke cracked: 'It wasn't me boss... the others started it.'

Fergie had his confession. He knew the guilty men. But how to punish them? That was the question.

He came up with a cracker... what do you do with eighteen-year-olds who play hide and seek? Easy – you make them sing nursery rhymes every morning for a week in front of the senior players!

One of the big regrets in Fergie's life is that he never got an official cap for Scotland... and that was down to one thing – meanness by the Scottish Football Association.

For Alex, a bustling centre forward with St Johnstone and Rangers, was drafted into the Scotland Far East Tour of 1967. They played several matches during the tour, but it was decreed that no caps would be given... for they cost £20 each!

Alex eventually led his country in a World Cup. He took over as Scotland's caretaker manager following the tragic death of Jock Stein in the 1986 campaign... and as usual the high jinks were part and parcel of the trip to Mexico.

The Scots prepared for Mexico in the high-altitude climate of Santa Fe, New Mexico, and the usual problems arose... notably what to do with the lads in their spare time. One popular diversion was a regular night out for a meal... with the squad breaking into several groups under supervision.

All was well until Fergie decided it was time the backroom boys had a night out on their own. All very well... but how do you make sure the players are behaving?

The first alarm bells should have rung when the trainer reported 'The lads will be fine... one hundred per cent.' Now any boss will tell you that is a danger sign... and so it proved for Fergie and his team.

After an enjoyable night out the backroom team arrived back at the hotel, and after a nightcap they retired to their rooms... but there was a shock in store for Scots physio Hugh Allen, who is of rather a dour nature. Fergie takes up the tale.

'Hugh had been responsible for transportation and safe keeping of the club kit hampers, which numbered about fifty-eight in total. What he didn't know was that, in his absence, the hampers had been given a new resting place... his room!

'Poor old Hugh, who isn't blessed with a great sense of humour, unlocked his door but was unable to open it because of the solid wicker basket wall which stood behind. This did absolutely nothing for his temperament as he scoured the players' rooms in search of the culprit. As expected, not one player knew anything about kit hampers, let alone the ones in Hugh's room.

'By this time I considered confiscating Hugh's bootlaces and tie as he looked on the verge of suicide. This must have been the most difficult task of my managerial career. Not administering discipline to the guilty party, but attempting to keep a straight face.

'Hugh continued to rant and rave until I eventually calmed him down and agreed to inspect the "damage", not realising that the room was impossible to enter. How did they get them in there, was the question posed. "Easy. Through the window" was Hugh's reply. "But you're on the second floor!" was mine. It was then I was struck by a thought. We were to face the might of South American teams who wouldn't think twice about ruining a player for life, but that was nothing compared to the risk of climbing up to Hugh's room.

'I left Hugh to find himself a bed for the night and returned to the sumptuous flat I had been given the use of. On the way over I had a good laugh to myself at Hugh's expense. The boot was soon to be on the other foot. Upon entering my apartment I discovered the lights weren't working. I thought, no, they wouldn't. Not to the manager. But they had! I entered the bedroom to find my bed half an inch from the ceiling. Underneath it were the hampers which hadn't been used on Hugh. Pinned to them was a note. "Guess who's been here. Signed, the phantom hamper."

'I bedded down for the night on the sofa and awoke the next morning surprisingly fresh for my experience which, as it turned out, had not finished. Not properly awake, I entered the bathroom to use the toilet. As I stood there I became aware of a rattling noise, similar to a drum. Unusual? Probably South American plumbing. Then, there was a wet feeling around my feet. I looked down and discovered cling film stretched across the toilet. Written on the cling film in felt-tip pen were the words, "He's been here too."

'The phantom had truly struck again!'

Chelsea manager Bobby Campbell, brought up in Liverpool's famous Scotland Road, has been one of the top coaches in British football for almost twenty-five years.

During his spells with top clubs such as QPR, Arsenal, Fulham, Portsmouth and now Chelsea, Bobby has coached some of the biggest names in football. Stars such as Alan Ball, George Best, Rodney Marsh, Stan Bowles, Bobby Moore, Gerry Francis, Don Givens, Liam Brady, David O'Leary, Frank Stapleton and latterly Mark Hateley and Neil Webb have all worked under Campbell

Bobby Campbell, Chelsea manager. A great coach who believes in the right things in the game

and benefited from the experience.

Campbell's philosophy on football is a simple one. All football has a strategy decided by the manager, but within that strategy players must be allowed to express themselves freely at all times.

In other words... be successful but have fun... and Bobby has had his share of both.

One of a family of twelve, he says, 'I laugh when I read today that deprivation is the main cause of lawlessness amongst youngsters. When I think back on the deprivation families shared in Scotland Road in my young days, it seems to me that today's youngsters don't know they're living.

'To say Scotland Road was tough is to say Shankly liked Liverpool. People lived four and five to a room at times, but the kids learned respect. If a policeman popped his head around the school playground gates after hours you'd see the fastest footballers ever. Even the slow players grew wings through fear of being caught playing football where we weren't supposed to and being reported to our parents.

'Cats with tails in our road were tourists... but we were brought up to appreciate life and our elders. I don't think it did any of us any harm.'

Life in such a community also fostered laughter, and Bobby still chuckles at how he got his first introduction to coaching.

'I was seventeen and captain of Liverpool Reserves and England's youth team. I was on a fabulous £5 per week and playing alongside men who had been my heroes at Anfield... players such as Bob Paisley, Billy Liddell and Phil Taylor.

'And it was Bob who put me on the coaching road. In those days at the end of every term at Liverpool University, well-known sports personalities used to visit the teachers' college to give a one-hour lecture a week on how teachers should instruct pupils on the school playing fields.

'Bob regularly got the job... but he didn't fancy it too much and one day he asked me to go in his place. I did and enjoyed it. The teachers-to-be enjoyed it too... I was asked back again and again in place of the great Paisley.

'Bob being Bob, he never quizzed me about the situation, but I can let him into a secret... it wasn't his football knowledge that let him down... it was his broad Geordie accent. The young teachers couldn't understand a word he was saying!'

Bobby's manager at Anfield in the early days was Don Welsh.

'We called him Coco the Clown,' grins Bobby. 'Not because he was a bad manager but because that was who he looked like – Coco the Clown... a bald head and big bushy eyebrows... a bit like old Bald Eagle himself, Jim Smith.'

And Bobby tells a lovely tale about Don Welsh and a giant Irish doorman called Paddy Walsh.

Now Paddy was a Liverpool docker, a fanatical Red who helped out by doing odd jobs at the club.

'Paddy used to tackle every job enthusiastically, and one day he was given the job of washing Don's car. Surrounded by buckets of soap suds and clear water he was giving the motor a real going over... watched by Bob Paisley.

'After a while old Bob gave me a shout. "Bobby son... go and tell Paddy that the boss wants him."

'I did as I was told and Paddy trooped off to the manager's office. Don Welsh of course knew nothing about the summons and a puzzled and angry Irishman was soon back at the car.

'Maybe it was anger that blinded him – I don't know – but what he didn't notice was that every window on the car had been wound down (by Bob Paisley of course) and Paddy gaily threw bucket after bucket of water at the car... before eventually realising in horror that water was pouring from every crevice and the inside was flooded.

'In the meantime Paisley and, I suspect, his partner in crime, Phil Taylor, were in stitches somewhere... and Don Welsh and a mad Irishman were hunting high and low for a young whippersnapper called Campbell.'

Bobby survived Big Paddy's wrath... which was a considerable feat in itself...

Top: The Football League v the Rest of the World – how many players can you name?; Graeme Souness *(above)*, no longer playing for Scotland but still battling, to put Rangers back on top; Alan Ball *(above right)*, as determined a manager as he was a player; and *(right)* Celtic manager Billy McNeill and assistant manager Tommy Craig – what a marvellous season for them!

and he even pulled off a remarkable con trick over him a year later along with a certain gentleman named Tarbuck.

Now Big Paddy was the doorman at the docks and was known as One-a-Day Walsh due to the fact that he would catch one docker a day trying to smuggle out stolen goods.

He was proud of his nickname and his alertness, but Campbell and Tarbuck – great mates – caught him out lovely.

Tarby, of course, was always Liverpool mad and used to walk through the players' entrance with Bobby pretending he was a player. Paddy probably was a bit suspicious at first – particularly when he never ever saw the bold Jim playing.

Bobby used to say: 'Great player that lad – pity about his knee injury.'

Eventually Tarby became so well known that Paddy was going around telling folk 'What a great young player that is ... shame he'll never make it big ... he's got a terrible leg!'

Bobby, a tough tackling wing-half, eventually had to give the game up himself at twenty-eight through injury but his interest and talent in coaching made him a natural for any backroom team and he began life as a coach ironically at Portsmouth under George Smith, who had been his England youth team coach. When Smith was sacked Bobby walked out too.

Soon after, he joined Queen's Park Rangers with Gordon Jago, and with talent such as Terry Venables, Phil Parkes, Gerry Francis, Stan Bowles and Rodney Marsh around, Loftus Road was a good – and fun – place to be.

Says Bobby: 'We had a marvellously talented squad with which we won the Second Division title ... Terry Venables was the skipper and in Rodney Marsh we had a ball artist supreme. We also had in the team a full back called Tony Hazel, who was a good solid pro but who was also the scapegoat for many a gag. Things happened to Tony, and Venables, Marsh and Co. didn't half play on it.

'On one occasion I was coaching the lads and expounding the use of the overlapping full back. Now Rodney Marsh could make a ball talk and would think nothing of taking four or five players solo before having a go at goal.

'During the coaching session Hazel, tired of making good runs and not getting the ball, complained. "Tell that Marsh to give me the ball, coach. He won't pass it to me."

'Rodney turned on me when I supported Tony and said, "Look ... I'd be better taking on three or four players in front of me than giving him the ball and relying on an accurate cross."'

As happens in football the very next match provided the opportunity to put practice into reality.

'Marsh got the ball in midfield and took on a couple of players and gave himself space. Now it so happens Tony Hazel had made a perfect run leaving him clear on the left. Rodney took time to look at the four men in front of him, then me, before sliding an inch-perfect ball to Hazel. On rushed Tony only to boot the ball high into the crowd behind the goal.

'At that point, Rodney rushed to the dug-out and shouted to me, "NOW will you ****ing well believe that I shouldn't give him the ball." I couldn't reply for laughing.'

From Rangers Bobby went on to coach Arsenal with Bertie Mee, and it was there with such as Ball, O'Leary, Brady, Rix and Stapleton under him that he enjoyed some great days.

'I remember Brady coming in as a sixteen-year-old. Tremendous talent. I christened him The Claw... for that was what that brilliant left peg of his reminded me of, it was so accurate. And then there was Bally, who was magnificent.

'Mind you he could drive you mad at times with his cheek. I remember one match where he had out-fought, out-thought and out-run the opposition. I told him, "They'll kick you off the park." He just grinned and said "Yeah, but they have to catch me first."'

At Fulham Bobby was manager and he took to Craven Cottage talent of the highest class... players such as George Best, Bobby Moore and Rodney Marsh.

Says Bobby: 'Bestie was the greatest talent I ever came across. I remember one match against Hereford he and Marsh really turned it on. I've never seen a dual performance like it. They seemed to want to outdo one another... and the skills they showed in ripping United apart will live with me forever.

'And you know I never had a bit of bother with the so-called "Jack The Lads" such as Bestie, Marsh and Bowles. They were marvellous in training and on the pitch for me. Their problems all seemed to come off the pitch... but they didn't let me down on it.

'And as for Bobby Moore... he was brilliant... one of the best professionals I ever came across. He never questioned a decision and was a real example to youngsters in his attitude to his work. I remember he once knocked on my door late in his career and asked me for some serious advice. It was one of the biggest accolades I've ever had.'

Before Chelsea Bobby was at Portsmouth, and, after taking them to the Second Division and earning them almost two million in transfer fees through his shrewd purchases of England-stars-to-be Mark Hateley and Neil Webb, he was rewarded with the sack. A ridiculous decision. Now he has the job of guiding Chelsea back into the First Division. He'll do it with style I'm sure... and a few laughs on the way.

Alan Ball – a
pocket dynamo

Saint

Billy McNeill, the man who last season guided Celtic to an historic League and Cup double in Scotland, has been part and parcel of the British soccer scene now for almost thirty years.

A gifted centre half and former captain of Scotland, he has also had managerial experience on both sides of the border... and knows full well the meaning of football fun.

The ordinary man in the street has no idea of the friendly rivalry that goes on between the English and the Scots at club level. The end-of-season Scotland–England international may not have quite the same impact with the general public as in days of old... but you can be sure that whoever loses that match will suffer at the hands of the Auld Enemy in the club dressing-rooms for the next twelve months.

And the rivalry stretches into management too.

Big Billy tells the lovely tale of how, when he was manager of Manchester City, he and fellow Scot Jimmy Frizzell used to do their damnedest to beat coaches Tony Book and Glynn Pardoe at everything from crosswords to tiddlywinks.

But one day the English had the last laugh.

England had qualified for the World Cup in Mexico on the previous evening, while Scotland had still to qualify....

As Billy sat in his Maine Road office a knock came at the door and when he opened it there were Book and Pardoe, all kitted out with sombreros and guitars serenading the big fellow with the England World Cup song!

Best, Osgood and Hudson – three more 'Jack the Lads', but they could play!

Laughs Billy: 'Needless to say they weren't asked for an encore.'

McNeill has always been a great believer in youth. His eye for talent stretches back to the great playing days with Celtic, when players such as Dalglish, Macari, Connelly, Hay and McGrain followed on the back of the great Lisbon Lions team he captained.

It's probably generally not known in England that Billy was also the man who gave Steve Archibald his big chance in senior football... with Clyde FC.

And Billy has two smashing stories about Archibald in those part-time days.

He says: 'Stevie in those days was, would you believe, a Rolls-Royce-trained mechanic, yet he was habitually late... always blaming the breakdowns of his ramshackle old car.

'He was an invaluable player to me at Clyde. He could play anywhere and frequently did... always doing a magnificent job.

'But what he doesn't know to this day is that I used to make compromises for him. While the rest of the squad were told to turn up at a certain time I would tell Stevie privately to turn up half an hour earlier... that made sure he'd be there at the same time as everyone else.

'Stevie deservedly has gone on to greater fame with Spurs, Barcelona and Scotland, but to my wife Liz he'll always be known as the kid with the squint jersey.

'Clyde were due to play Celtic in a Glasgow Cup tie and we had a new strip delivered. As luck would have it we discovered belatedly that there was no number 8 on Steve's jersey.

'Liz came to the rescue with needle and thread... but the repair job wasn't perfect... which didn't please the image-conscious Steve too much.

'"The number's squint," said Stevie. "Too bad," said Liz. "Get out and play," said I.

'It couldn't have happened in Barcelona.'

Now as a Scot I'm well aware the nightmare New Year can turn out to be for football managers. We Scots do like to celebrate at Hogmanay, and Big Billy found out that the passing years do not diminish players yearning for a good time at Ne'erday when he was manager of Aberdeen.

He explains: 'We had a New Year's Day game with Dundee United coming up and I wanted everything to be right. We were on a good run and I was determined that it would continue... I didn't want any Hogmanay nonsense from anyone.

'I thought I was clever putting two young flat-sharing bachelors – Willie Garner and Bobby Glennie – into a friend's boarding house over Hogmanay.

'Imagine my surprise when in the wee sma' hours the pair, who had obviously been overdoing the celebrations, phoned me at home to wish me a Happy New Year.

'I told them: "Don't worry about wishing me all the best. Worry about yourselves tomorrow."

'In the morning I dropped the two of them, and instead of playing in the big North East derby they had to travel to the back of beyond with the reserves for a friendly match against a Highland junior side.

'Scottish hospitality is one thing... Scottish stupidity another.'

In his playing days with Celtic, Billy often found himself in Ireland on pre-season tours... Jock Stein reckoned the gentle Irish way and non-contact friendly matches were the ideal way for his men to tune up for a season.

And one habitual visitor was a Celtic-daft Irish priest called Dr Sheridan, who always turned up on cue and attached himself to the Parkhead party whenever it arrived on the Emerald Isle.

Says Billy: 'Eventually everyone – players, directors and Big Jock – got used to him being around.

'Well, one day we were playing a pre-season friendly at Limerick at a dog track, and for a team which had recently won the European Cup we were absolute murder.

'Half-time couldn't have come quick enough for the Big Man. He slammed the dressing-room door shut and gave us a right earful... storming on about maintaining standards, etc.

'In the middle of the tirade the door burst open and in came Father Sheridan to tell us where he thought we were going wrong. Big Jock at first tried to head him off politely... but the good doctor was determined to have his say.

'Finally, Jock could stand no more. As we waited in anticipation he blew storming at the priest: "Look, father! I wouldn't walk into your church and take over your pulpit. SO GET LOST... AND GIVE US PEACE!"

'The room erupted... that was the end of our dressing down. Even Big Jock knew there was no way back after that classic.'

Like Billy I learned to respect Jock Stein... although there is no doubt that he was a real wily old fox.

The story is told that, when Celtic played Inter Milan in that never-to-be-forgotten European Cup final in Lisbon in 1967, he twice upstaged the great Helenio Herrera, then rated the top manager in world football.

Celtic were underdogs, but as the teams came out together Stein began to sing the Celtic song and his players followed suit. Suddenly the Italians were unsettled.

And they were even more put out when Stein and his backroom team grabbed the bench Herrera had wanted. Psychology is

Greavsie

important in football. Little touches like that make teams worry.

I suppose it's the equivalent of two heavyweight boxers attempting to psyche one another out with those stone eyeball encounters at the beginning of a title fight.

Herrera certainly found out that day that Stein was soccer heavyweight of the highest class. Celtic went on to beat Inter 2–1 to become the first British side ever to win the European Cup.

And, finally, here's a gem I can't resist including.

When West Germany were in Mexico preparing for the 1970 World Cup, a lady of the night visited several of the players' rooms. Each time when she asked for payment for services rendered, she was referred to a certain room number.

When she called to collect the cash, she wakened up the West German team manager Helmut Schon.

His reply isn't fit for print.

9 THE SHOWBIZ CONNECTION

Football and showbusiness go hand in hand. Both provide entertainment for the masses and both artistes and players love their own particular stage. We both count many showbusiness people amongst our friends and have found them to be amongst the biggest football fanatics. Their love of the game and sense of fun has brought in millions of pounds from charity matches all over Britain, and here some of them look back on their own special moments in football and the fun it gives them.

Saint

I'll start with Jimmy Tarbuck because he's been part of my life since those marvellous days of the sixties when he bounced on to the stage of the London Palladium with a Beatle haircut and a line of Liverpool patter never heard before to become an overnight sensation.

Tarby of course is Liverpool Red through and through and never lets anyone forget it. Elsewhere in this book Chelsea manager Bobby Campbell tells how a young Tarby would walk through the players' entrance with him at Anfield posing as a player. At times he seemed part of our squad... his infectious laugh and quickfire gags giving us a gee-up whenever we needed one.

The great Tarbuck – a football legend in his own mind!

There's no doubt in my mind that Jimmy would have put aside his fabulous success as an entertainer if he could have become a Liverpool player. As it is he has been part and parcel of the Anfield scene for almost thirty years... and some of his stories are priceless.

Like the time he played against a Shanks team at Anfield. It happened in the early seventies. The occasion – a testimonial match for our iron-hard full back Gerry Byrne... the hardest tackler I've ever seen in football.

Over 40,000 fans turned out to pay tribute to Gerry and part of the entertainment was a special match between Tarby's team and a Shanks select.

Now Tarby as I've mentioned had always dreamed of playing in the coveted red shirt, and with such greats as Billy Liddell, Tom Finney, Bert Trautmann, Bobby Murdoch and Kenny Lynch in his side (now how did Lynchy get in that line-up?) he thought that his side and not Shanks's might wear the red jerseys.

The request went in to Shanks via Bob Paisley and the retort came back: 'He bloody wants to play in the Liverpool shirts? Well so do I.'

Inevitably Shanks's lot wore red and Tarby's yellow!

Jimmy tells a lovely Shanks story from during the game:

'Half-way through Shanks's lot were awarded a penalty... and there was no doubt at all who would be taking it.

'The great man picked up the ball and with the Kop screaming "Shankly – Shankly" he put on his best Cagney act. He hitched up his pants and hit the ball sweet and low to Bert Trautmann's left-hand side.

'Bert, though, was marvellously agile and he not only got down to save, he got his whole body behind the ball... a wonderful save and one in the eye for Shanks.

'But the old boy never could accept that someone had got one over on him.

'As the teams left the pitch he sidled up to Trautmann and growled "Aye Bert – I had you going the wrong way with that one... didn't I?"'

Now Tarbuck in those sixties fun days travelled everywhere with Liverpool and one weekend we were due to play Arsenal on the Saturday and Spurs on the Monday.

We duly beat Arsenal and Shanks decided that we should stay down in Luton... but on no account was anyone to go out for a drink at night.

Jimmy, though, gave myself and Ron Yeats the nod that his big mate, Johnny Speight the scriptwriter, was having cocktails at his place and we were invited... that's if we could escape our hotel.

At around nine o'clock big Ron and I decided to gamble... by getting out of the back door. At the far end of the hotel garden was a wall and naturally Ron being the big fellow and me the small one he gave me a leg up. In fact it was more than a leg up. I was balancing precariously on his shoulders ready to jump down onto the road outside when suddenly I heard two unmistakable voices... those of Shanks and Bob Paisley. As I balanced above them the boss and Bob stood underneath talking about watching out for anyone trying to beat the curfew. As Yeatsy cottoned on to what was happening, I was standing astride his shoulders, which were heaving with laughter. Shanks was in danger of getting a fellow Scot on his head... and I was in danger of getting the biggest rocket of all time!

Luckily for me the pair walked on... and Ron and I headed back for the hotel... no drinks for us that night!

The next day of course Tarby was doubled up at the story. 'Serves you right you rascals,' was all the sympathy we got from him.

Now Jimmy has always fancied himself as a footballer, and like most Liverpudlians he is comfortable on the ball. Years of playing with tennis balls in the streets as a kid has left its mark. And over the years he has helped raise fortunes for charity by appearing in Showbiz Eleven matches for some cause or other.

But in one match he was a bigger smash than he bargained for.

Explains Jimmy: 'It was a wet, miserable day at Beaconsfield and we were shooting in before a charity match.

'Someone knocked the ball over and I hit a high dipping shot over the crossbar.

'Now the ball was heavy and solid and I'd hit it hard. It fell like a rock... and smashed straight through a parked car's windscreen.

'The lads all laughed, and being a "Jack The Lad" I scoffed – serves the bugger right for parking there.

'Then they told me, "The laugh's on you Jim – that's the referee's car!"

'A few minutes later out came the referee raging that he wanted compensation for the damage. "Not likely – it was an act of God," said I.

'Mind you he got his own back . . . he never gave our lot one decision and I had to be on my best behaviour – he was ready to give me my marching orders.'

Tarby was also involved in one of our funniest wind-ups . . . against my old Scotland team-mate, the great Jim Baxter.

Jimmy, Ron Yeats and myself were in a London hotel before Scotland played England at Wembley in 1967. England were world champs and Scotland according to the press had no chance. Mind you with Baxter in your team you always had a chance.

For a bit of mischief Ron and I got Jimmy to telephone Baxter at the Scotland team hotel masquerading as *Mirror* sports writer Sam Leitch. The conversation went like this:

Tarby: 'Jim you've always done well at Wembley before, are you confident you can do as well this time?'

Baxter: 'Of course Sam – I always like playing against the English.'

Tarby: 'Yes Jim, but don't you think the big Wembley pitch will be a bit too much for you now?'

Baxter: 'What do you mean by that?'

Tarby: 'Well let's face it Jimmy you're not as quick as you used to be are you?'

Baxter, getting audibly irate: 'What makes you say that?'

Tarby: 'You used to be called Slim Jim – you couldn't call yourself that anymore . . . it must be likely that those quick English

forwards will rip the pants off you . . .'

A fuming Baxter: 'You cheeky ****ing *******. You just ***ing well wait until tomorrow to see if I can still do it you ****.'

At that point Tarby, myself and Big Ron were howling with laughter and I could hear Slim Jim on the other end of the phone suddenly realising the wind-up.

'Wait till I get my hands on you . . . I know who it is, it's St John, Yeats and Tarbuck . . . you cheeky *******.'

Jim of course saw the funny side . . . and he also lived up to his word. The next day at Wembley he put on a display rated by Greavsie as one of the greatest virtuoso performances seen at Wembley since the fabulous Ferenc Puskas destroyed England in the fifties. Scotland in the end became the first team to inflict a defeat on the new world champions . . . they won 3–2.

It's interesting listening to Tarbuck on Liverpool. He has watched all the great Anfield teams and personalities and being a star himself says 'Liverpool's greatest asset is not having a star system. Shanks began that with his team imposing the fact that the game was bigger than any player and that teamwork was all. Every Liverpool side through the years has retained that belief and that is why they are successful – no player is more important than any other.'

Mind you Jimmy does have one favourite player in all the years he's supported the Reds: 'Kenny Dalglish to my mind has been the greatest,' says Tarby. 'To my mind he was Liverpool's greatest ever signing after Shanks . . . wonderful commitment, skill and insight. I only wish the Scottish public had appreciated him as much as the Kop.'

Tarby's Football Funny: Bruce Grobbelaar was making his debut for Liverpool at Anfield. The Kop were hailing Bob Paisley when the opposing centre forward sent in a rocket of a shot from thirty yards. The ball cracked back off the crossbar and the striker running in met the ball flush on his forehead. The ball was heading for the top left-hand corner of the net when Brucie somehow finger-tipped the ball over. A match-winning save and Liverpool went on to win 1-0.

At the end the striker sought out Bruce and said: 'Jesus that was some save that one. I've never hit a ball so hard in my life.'

To which Bruce answered: 'To be perfectly honest mate – I was going for the first one!'

———————— o ————————

Another football fan from the showbiz world is the immensely talented Eddie Large... the heavier half of the Little and Large comedy duo.

Eddie is a rabid Manchester City fan – despite the fact that he originally hails from another hotbed of football, Glasgow.

In fact Eddie was brought up in Oatlands, just a stone's throw away from a ground I knew well in my early days... Shawfield, home at that time of Clyde FC.

In those days Tommy Ring, the famous Scottish left-winger, was Eddie's hero, and it was Tommy's picture Eddie took south when his family moved to Maine Road when he was ten years old.

Eddie's Glasgow upbringing served him well in his new surroundings. He says: 'In Glasgow I did nothing else but play football day in day out, and by the time I reached Manchester I was a dab hand at the game.'

Eddie was in fact so good at football that he got himself the job of cricket captain at his school... Claremont Road Primary.

He explains: 'I got chosen for the football team near the end of the season... there were only two games left and we won 4-0 and 2-0 and I scored every goal.

'I was suddenly a star and they reckoned "If he's good at football he must be good at cricket." Nobody thought to tell them that they don't go in much for cricket in Scotland... that was a game for cissies... and so when I turned out at cricket I was a complete disaster. Mind you they still let me play in the football team and that was good enough for me.'

In fact Eddie matured to be a first-class player and he was chosen at seventeen for the England Boys Club squad to play Scotland at Easter Road.

Says Eddie: 'It was good news and bad news. The good news was that I was chosen... the bad news was that I would have to tell my Dad, who was a died-in-the-wool Scot, that I had been picked for England.

'In fact I got off the hook... albeit painfully. Before the match I fell off a bicycle and was run over by a bus. That was the end of my football career.'

Being brought up in Maine Road there was only one team for Eddie: 'I didn't realise there was another team in Manchester called United. All my mates were City fans and I was soon Blues mad too.'

Eddie has never lost his affection for City. He still watches them whenever possible and over the years has regularly given the Maine Road players a pre-match lift with his marvellous impressions.

On one occasion though it could have cost him his marriage.

Explains Eddie: 'It was when City played Spurs in the FA Cup Final in 1981.

'I had promised my wife a sunshine holiday in Florida, but as the lads progressed in the Cup I was getting twitchy... and when they won the semi-final, suddenly it was Marbella not Florida for the family...

Spain, you see, is not too far from Wembley.

'John Bond was the manager of City and I had everything fixed. I was to meet the team bus before Wembley Way and travel in with the lads. Quite an honour.

'And what a job I had to get there. From Marbella to Malaga, Malaga to Madrid and Madrid to Heathrow. A taxi to the head of Wembley Way... and there I was like a prune with my head out as the coach approached, only for it to drive right by. That motorcycle escort was stopping for no-one.

'I then had to leg it up Wembley Way to catch the coach... and was puffed out by the time I caught up with Bondie and the lads. I made it though and got in for the pre-match preamble. I had a bit of fun with the lads, and without looking at the ticket John had given me began to make my way out.

'"Look at the ticket you clown," said Bondie... and I did. It was for the players' bench. I spent the most wonderful afternoon of my life sitting amongst the players as City drew 2-2 with Spurs in one of the best finals in years.

'At the end of it though it was a replay, and with the wife browning herself back in Marbella there was no way I could stay.

'I ended up the following Thursday morning watching the replay in a bar in Marbella on television... with a Radio Four commentary blasting away on a transistor. The locals thought I was mad as I jumped up and down as the goals kept going in. In the end of course Ricky Villa scored a fabulous winner for Spurs... maybe it was just as well I wasn't on the bench for that one.'

Eddie now knows of course that there is another team in Manchester, and admits that last season he was close to being drummed out of the Blues club for aiding and abetting, of all people, United manager Alex Ferguson.

He says: 'It was the day City played Liverpool in the FA Cup at Maine Road. We got a right good thumping and I was driving out of the ground feeling a bit umpty when I saw this figure flag me down.

'It was Alex Ferguson. His car had broken down and he needed a lift. I said: "All right, but only if you don't tell anybody."

'Naturally I had to help, but I was aware that if any City fans saw me I was in dead trouble. I gave Fergie his lift, but to save face I kept my head so low behind the wheel people must have thought the car was driving itself.

'Fergie had this big grin on his face. He knew the score... but I made it in the end... the City players still talk to me.'

Eddie's Football Funny: Big Jim, a life-long Manchester City fan, died near the end of a season. He had left instructions that he must see every City game, so his family had him embalmed and stuck him in the stand for the next game.

'Trouble was City played so badly he left the ground at half-time asking the way to the nearest crematorium.'

—————— O ——————

Another talented entertainer who could play a bit in his day is Jerry Stevens. Jerry played for Notts County in the fifties as a speedy left winger. His football career ended when a County director found out he was singing with a band as well as playing football.

'We can't have our lads up until one o'clock in the morning in dance halls – they should be in their beds by ten o'clock,' he proclaimed as the team returned from Port Vale.

Jerry, by this time a regular performer with the band and earning more as a singer than a footballer, promptly gave the game up... although he continued to play amateur football with the Sheffield Club... recognised as the oldest football club in the world.

Jerry has also turned out regularly with the Showbiz Eleven, making a mint for charity, and he remembers his days with them with affection.

'Jess Conrad has run the Showbiz Eleven for many years and is the regular goalkeeper. Now it's well known that Jess is one of the biggest poseurs of all time and it became a joke amongst the lads to look out for the instant replay after any goalmouth incident involving Jess.

'No – it wasn't a replay of Jess's saves we looked for. It was him moving quick as lightning for his comb after he had kicked the ball clear... he couldn't live with himself unless not a hair was out of place.'

Jerry also remembers a game where Greavsie had the comedians in stitches. It happened ten years ago when Jimmy guested for the Showbiz Eleven against a Dennis Waterman Select.

'At the time Robert Powell was one of the biggest stars in showbusiness. He had just starred as Jesus Christ in *The Greatest Story Ever Told* and was a household name all over the world.

'But Robert suddenly found himself on the wrong end of a tough tackle and down he went injured. The referee blew the whistle, but before he could call on a trainer Greavsie chirped up: "You don't need a trainer for him referee... he can cure himself!"'

Jerry's Football Funny: Who played for Chelsea at Stamford Bridge on Boxing Day morning 1952 and for West Ham at Upton Park on the same afternoon?

Answer: The Band of the Coldstream Guards.

Another funny man who loves his football is big Mike Burton the Merseyside comedian who sprang to fame on that great TV show *The Comedians* in the seventies and who is now one of the most sought-after comics in theatres and clubs.

Mike was brought up in Birkenhead and describes himself as a 'mean wing half'.

'St Hughes was my school... called after Yosser you know,' he gags. 'The football fields were steeped in blood... mainly mine. You see from the age of three I had to wear heavy glasses... couldn't see a blooming thing without them so I'd often kick my own players... and got a good kicking back.'

Big Mike enjoys poking fun at himself but in fact he was fairly useful. His best mate Kenny Birch went on to play for Everton and it was suggested Mike should train with the Blues... but he had this eyesight problem, you see!

Mike does admit to having had three football loves... Tranmere Rovers, Everton and Liverpool.

'I got the best of three worlds,' says Mike.

'I used to join the other nutters in the Cowshed at Tranmere and had a lot of fun.

'I remember one freezing winter's night watching a match with Darlington. The floodlights were none too clever and it was getting dark when the cry went up from the bench: "We need some white balls." To which one wag shouted: "Well don't look at me mate, mine are blue with the bloody cold!"

'Eventually I gave up the Cowshed though... I got fed up with the rust falling on me every time the ball hit the roof.

'So I moved over to Goodison thinking... now for some action. And I spent three seasons of sheer misery. Every time I went the score was nil-nil... and some of the time Everton were lucky to get nil!'

Mike eventually learned sense and now watches Liverpool whenever possible, saying: 'During my Tranmere and Everton days it was a blessing my eyesight was so bad. Now it's costing me a fortune... I keep getting new specs just to make sure the football I'm watching isn't a mirage.'

One football memory Mike still chuckles at is the day he played alongside Sir Alf Ramsey and Nat Lofthouse.

'I was in Jersey in summer season and the Portuguese waiters challenged some of us to a match on the beach at St Helier. I knew Alf and Nat were staying in the next hotel and asked them to join in on the side of we Brits.

'God bless them... they did. But the next day there was something like forty-a-side on the beach and as usual I was getting stuck in with the best of them, running my guts out, until I noticed Sir Alf and Nat beckoning me back down field.

'"Stay here with us," they said. "Why?" said I. "Because we don't want to see you get killed," said the old pros. They weren't bad judges either.'

———————— o ————————

Frank Carson is another funny man who loves his football... although he admits: 'I'm an Irish jinx. Every team I get involved with gets that sinking feeling. I was once allowed in the Liverpool dressing-room before a game to give the boys a few laughs... they promptly lost to Spurs and I was never invited back.

'I was a director of Newport County and look what happened to them. Now I'm a director of Colchester United and every time I've been to see them they've been beaten. Now I'm banned from home games.'

Frank was bitten by the soccer bug in his early days as a teenager in Belfast.

'I played for Belfast Boys Club and because of the religious differences the team had to be made up of fifty per cent Catholics and fifty per cent Protestants... now only we Irish could work out how to get half and half out of eleven. I was the oddball... so they stuck me in goal!

'And I remember well my last game for them... they took me out of goal with the score 21-1... for the other lot. I was arguing with the referee... I reckoned one of the goals was offside. "That was never a goal referee," I pleaded.

'All he said was "Read the paper in the morning son."'

After giving the game up Frank started to follow Belfast Celtic, and he tells a story about Alisha Scott, the ex-Liverpool great.

'Alisha was manager at the time, and being a real professional himself he expected his own players to toe the line. Now our keeper at the time was Hughie Kelly, who was known to like a night out.

'One Saturday Alisha found out that Hughie had been on the bevvy the night before and when Hughie let in a goal he was immediately rounded on after the game: "As for you Kelly... what a goal to let in... I tell you my granny could have saved that one."

'A week later Alisha put up the team sheet for the following match and Kelly, a right lad, rubbed out his name at the top of the sheet and pencilled in "ALISHA SCOTT'S GRANNY"!'

Over the years Big Frank has been a great supporter of Scottish football and has often appeared in charity shows on behalf of both Celtic and Rangers supporters' clubs and boys' clubs.

In fact he must be the only person ever to be awarded the honours of Patron of the Celtic Boys Club and also Life Member of the Rangers Supporters Club. Believe me you have to be pretty special to achieve that double!

Frank through the years became very friendly with the late great Jock Stein and he even found time to cheer the Big Man up in his darkest hours... following his near fatal car crash on the A74 in 1975.

Frank was on his way to Scotland when he heard about the car crash and dropped into the hospital to visit Stein. The doctor, though, would not allow any visitors as Big Jock was gravely ill.

However, he fought his way through the crisis and awoke to find a telegram from Carson at his bedside reading 'St Peter very annoyed you didn't turn up!'

Knowing Jock Stein, he would have chuckled at that.

Mind you I doubt if the Big Man would have chuckled at another of Carson's capers... for he actually recommended Kenny Dalglish to Sir Matt, Busby when he was manager of Manchester United.

Says Frank: 'I'd seen this kid playing with a Celtic junior side and thought he was wonderful. I told Sir Matt but nothing was ever done... thank God... Big Jock would have killed me if he'd lost him.'

Frank still chuckles at one typical bit of Stein humour.

'I asked Jock, "Aren't you worried about the challenge from Rangers, Big Man?" Quick as a flash he answered, "Frank they've got nothing on their sideboard but polish."'

Recently Frank was guest at a big dinner in Glasgow to honour Kenny Dalglish.

'It was a very mixed company with a lot of businessmen and Dougie Donnelly, the BBC sports presenter, was MC.

'Now I now Kenny comes in for a bit of stick from the media down south for his Glasgow accent, but I couldn't believe what happened in Glasgow.

'Dougie asked us all to watch and listen to a video tape where first a Yugoslav was talking, then a Latvian and then a Frenchman. Now obviously we couldn't understand a word. I was wondering what the gag was until Dougie then put on a tape of Kenny talking... and still no-one could understand a word! The place was in uproar... but Kenny took it well.'

One story almost in reverse once happened to the late great Scottish sports writer Hughie Taylor, then of the *Daily Record*.

Celtic's assistant manager under Jock Stein in the golden days was Sean Fallon, a hard-tackling full back who hailed from Sligo in the Republic.

Now Sean has lived in Scotland for almost forty years, but it's fair to say that he's never quite lost his broad Irish brogue. In fact one still has to listen intently to understand Sean, who, by the way, is a marvellous man.

One year Celtic took on a friendly against Sean's hometown team Sligo Rovers, and at the after-match banquet Sean was the guest of honour.

Sean duly made a nice little speech and was heartily applauded – he being one of Sligo's favourite sons – although as Hughie Taylor told it not many of the Scottish party understood a word.

Hughie almost choked on his Scotch when one of the local parish priests sitting next to him turned and said: 'You know we're all very proud of our Sean's achievements... there's only one thing... hasn't he got a terrible Glasgow accent?'

Frank's Football Funny: It's a true story. I once went to a Celtic–Rangers Old Firm derby match at Parkhead accompanied by Bobby Robson, who was then manager of Ipswich Town.

'We were taken to the match by a friend of

mine… Tim Kelly… who used to be one of the top men at the Central Hotel in Glasgow.

'Now in the back of the estate wagon Tim had two huge Doberman Pinschers, and I tell you I wasn't too happy with those two brutes sitting at the back eyeing me up.

'Anyway as usual when we tried to park outside Celtic Park a street urchin arrived and offered: "Watch your car for fifty pence mister."

'At that Tim pointed to the two huge dogs and said: "Listen son, see these dogs… they're vicious animals. I don't need anyone to guard my car with those two in the back. Anyone goes near them they'd eat them alive… so you be careful… keep away."

'Off we went to the match and when we returned Bobby Robson and I were soon doubled up with laughter while Tim was tearing his hair out. For on his windscreen was a note from the kid saying: "Hope your Dobermans can blow up tyres mister!"

'The little rascal had let every one of Tim's tyres down!'

Greavsie

I've a question to ask – how come Liverpool has collared all the best footballers and the best comedians?

It's only when you sit down to write an article on the showbiz connections in foot-ball that you realise how many Liverpudlians light up our lives from the stages of Britain.

Traditionally of course Liverpool hogs the market on comics. That quickfire Scouse patter makes them natural comedians. And their love of football is in-bred. The dark recesses of Scotland Road and the like bred a

121

wit that defies adversity. They also produced a breed of tennis-ball footballers whose love of the game is second to none.

Like Saint I salute the showbusiness boys for the work they have done for charity in this country. The Variety Club has supplied Sunshine Coaches for deprived and handicapped kids throughout Britain through charity concerts, sports events and football matches... and the stories surrounding some of our best-known entertainers are hilarious.

Have you heard for instance the one about the showbiz star who spent his wedding night sleeping with a football team? Impossible? Not when you're football mad Stan Boardman – that laugh-a-minute Scouse comic with a million gags about 'The Jairmans'.

Now Stan was a fine player in his young days... he actually played for Liverpool's 'A' team just before Bill Shankly took over at Anfield, and I'm told he was equally useful at centre-half or centre forward.

As Shanks moved into Anfield young Stan moved into the army, and by the time he had come out Shanks had pruned the playing staff from fifty to nineteen... and Stan was one of the unfortunate ones.

But football is still in his blood and he remembers well his training days at Melwood – Liverpool's training ground. He says: 'The facilities consisted of half a dozen large tin baths in a wooden hut. We 'A' team players used to cram into the baths three at a time.'

Changed days indeed.

But back to the wedding day story.

Stan takes up the tale: 'I had got myself involved with Skelmersdale the year they made the Amateur Cup Final at Wembley – which incidentally was the year Saint trained them – and I was due to get married

in London at eleven in the morning on the same day as the final.

'I duly made an honest woman of Vivienne and then as she and the rest of the guests headed back to the hotel for the reception I said: "Ta-ta I'm off to Wembley!"

'As you can imagine I wasn't exactly top of the pops. In fact Vivienne could have strangled me, but there was no way I was missing my mates playing at Wembley.

'As it happened they drew 0–0 after extra time with Enfield. Alan Birmingham missed a penalty for us and at the end I was commiserating with the lads. Naturally I told them to come along and visit us if stuck... never thinking they would take me up on the offer.

'I legged it back to our reception... amazingly the new missus was still there, and I was just calming everyone down when there was a knock on the door. It was the lads and naturally they had to have a bevvy. They stayed. We all got drunk and I ended up spending my wedding night sleeping on the floor with most of the Skelmersdale football team while my new bride slept in her bed.'

Amazing to think that Stan is still happily married to the same lady isn't it?

As someone who has sampled non-league football with Barnet I know the fun that exists outside League football... and so does Stan.

'When I moved on from Liverpool I took up with an old mate, Tommy Jones, who played for Everton and Wales. Tommy was manager of Rhyl and he asked me to join them. It was one of the best moves I ever made. I had more laughs with Tommy and the lads than I've had at the Palladium.

'The club of course was run on a shoestring and full of Scousers who were as wide as the Mersey. We used to get paid £5 a game and we soon realised that if there was not a big

crowd in, then last man up stood to get nothing at all.

'So myself and one or two other Scousers used to count the crowd. If it was small and Tommy had only gathered £25 we would hang back while the others had their bath. We'd get our money before it ran out... and then we were off like a shot into Liverpool. The others might have been clean... they were also skint!'

Stan also remembers how at times a bath was sorely needed.

He explains: 'It was in the early days of

floodlights and we had lights of a sort at Rhyl but didn't have the new white balls to go with them.

'So Tommy Jones used to have a bucket of whitewash ready to whiten the old leather balls. And when we were playing in winter every time the ball came near the dug-out he would splosh the ball into the bucket.

'Out on the field of course we were all heading the ball and when we came in at full time we were dripping whitewash. We looked like a team of ghosts.'

One thing I remember well about my

Barnet days... the stick we non-leaguers took when we didn't perform well... and Stan still bears the scars from similar débâcles.

'We were playing in the Welsh Cup at some village in Wales and before the game we had to help the locals clear a flock of sheep off the pitch.

'Maybe our exertions took too much out of us, but we finished up getting slaughtered 4-0, and after the match Tommy Jones raged at us "You were all bloody murder... we'd have been better letting the sheep play for us."'

Stan's great gags about the Germans of course have made him a household name in Britain, but not many people know that he hit on the theme by actually playing for a German football team. While playing for the army in Germany he was noticed by a football scout and wound up playing for Badlipspring in one of the lesser leagues.

'It was great fun,' says Stan. 'But I couldn't understand a word they said. But after a week or two I had them all at it shouting: "Gimme the ball Wack!"'

'Actually it was during that time I noticed the Germans' habits and when I went into showbusiness I started to describe them... and that's how "The Jairmans" jokes all started.'

Stan of course has a wealth of football gags... with Everton his favourite whipping boys.

He says: 'There was this Red who had a wonderful dog he took to Anfield with him. And when Liverpool scored the dog did three somersaults and a belly flop. When they scored twice it stood on its back paws and did a back flip.

'The bloke next to him was amazed and asked: "What happens when Everton score?" Back came the reply: "It does half a dozen somersaults and four back flips." "That's fantastic – how does he manage that?" asks the fan. "Because I give it the biggest kick up the backside you've ever seen," the Red replies.'

I had a dog like that once.

Then there's Stan's favourite Tranmere Rovers gag. Now as any Merseysider will tell you, Rovers are the area's Cinderella club. They're well loved by the locals but usually skint and surviving on thin air.

Stan tells the story of how one season the Tranmere directors got together and as an incentive decided to give any player who scored a goal £100.

The season wears on and Rovers cannot score a goal. Finally they get to their last home match and the centre forward, late in the game, gathers the ball in midfield, beats four opponents, draws the keeper and smacks home a beauty.

To a man the four directors jump to their feet and roar 'Offside referee – offside!'

No Stan Boardman contribution though would be complete without a 'Jairman' joke and sure enough he has one: 'Did you hear the one about the German striker who scored three goals... the next day in the paper it was described as a Gerry-at-trick!'

———————— O ————————

Another showbusiness great who loves his football is that funny man Russ Abbott, who to my mind is the most hilarious guy on television these days... apart from the Saint that is!

Now Russ, I have to stress, is not a Liverpudlian. He comes from just down the road at Chester and he admits that there are two teams in his life - Chester and, would you believe, Liverpool. You know I'm sure the Saint is paying all these stars to claim allegiance to his beloved Reds!

Anyone who has watched Russ in action in charity football matches will agree that he is every bit as funny off the stage as on it.

Russ admits to being a goalkeeper all his life.

'I played for the school in goal you know... we won 28–1 and I got suspended... for letting in that one goal.

'We were playing in a country village and if we were not using the pitch the local cows were. Naturally the goalposts were their gathering place... they loved to rub themselves against the wood.

'But cows being cows, there were more than a few cowpats in the goalmouth and I wasn't diving in amongst that lot for anyone.

'Anyway we were miles ahead when this soft shot comes my way... there was no way I wanted to cover myself in cow dung so I tried to stop it with my foot. The ball beat me and ended up in the net... and my schoolmaster promptly suspended me from the football team for not diving to save the goal.

'I suppose one way or another I ended up in the mumble mumble after all!'

Russ has often turned out for the Showbiz XI during summer season in Blackpool and he always gives the fans a real treat.

All the visual brilliance we see on television is brought to life as he dresses up in long shorts, roll-neck sweater and hooker down cap in the best Bert Trautmann style. His antics are hilarious as those long rubber legs of his go into action... and despite all the hilarity he's not a bad keeper either.

His old-style gear really does take a trick and he now has the full outfit... right down to a pair of size ten Mansfield Hotspur boots in mint condition.

Russ says: 'How I got them was amazing really. I went on Red Rose Radio in Blackpool to promote a charity match and mentioned if anyone out there had any Mansfield Hotspurs could they please send them on. It was a gag of course, but next day a bloke turned up at the stage door with a pair of brand new boots.

'He had taken over a shoe store in Blackpool and while clearing out a press he came across a pair of the old original toe bashers... and they were my size too.

'I was delighted, but the next day I was hobbling with pain for real while the crowd thought I was up to my usual nonsense. For I hadn't done what every good lad used to do all those years ago... coat the monsters with dubbin and soak them in a tub of water. I was crippled, but the crowd thought I was playing it all for laughs.'

Russ, a quiet man off screen, does love a gag, and one of his best while playing in Blackpool used to be to bring on one of the elephants from the famous Tower Circus and lay it along his goal line. Then he would challenge the opposition to score.

And of course Blunderwoman, alias Bella Emberg, had to make an entrance usually to give the big fellow the kiss of life following a particularly daring save....

'We used to bring on guys on stilts as well,' says Russ. 'They weren't so good on the ground but magic in the air!'

One of Russ's biggest memories was playing for Liverpool alongside Saint, Ron Yeats and Tommy Smith against Blackpool in a charity match at Bloomfield Road back in 1983.

'Tommy Smith was nice to me... he only growled at me once. And we won 3-2 despite me being in goal. I enjoyed it immensely... but I still have nightmares at some of those Tommy Smith tackles.'

So do I, Russ. So do I.

———————— o ————————

Finally a few stories about another old mucker of mine... from the old days at West Ham... the Black Pearl himself, no not Eusebio - Kenny Lynch.

Now Lynchy is one of the greatest characters in British showbusiness. He's always on hand to help in any charity event, and being a sports nut is ever ready to compete in any sport that brings in cash for the needy.

Boxing and golf are his greatest loves, but he has turned out on many occasions for the Showbiz XI, and like Russ Abbott he remembers schooldays as a budding goalkeeper.

'Actually my career was nipped in the bud at a very early age,' grins Kenny.

'I was around nine or ten when I was picked in goal for the school team. My brother Teddy, who played reserve football for Charlton Athletic, came to watch... and I let in eighteen goals.

'After the eighteenth went in the teacher pulled me out of goal and tried me up front and I scored two. We finished up losing 20-2, but that was the end of a promising career as a footballer.'

Kenny in fact turned to boxing and became a useful fighter at feather and bantamweight, but he couldn't get away from football. Being an East End kid he naturally supported West Ham and he, like myself, counts Bobby Moore as one of his best friends.

'Mooro used to encourage me to play in the Showbiz matches and I loved them. They were great fun. I remember one day playing in front of 40,000 people with Sir Stanley Matthews on my right and the great Tom Finney on my left. Somehow I was picked to play for Old England... against the Showbiz XI, and Stan and Tom kept beating everyone and laying the ball on for me in front of goal. I kept popping the ball into the net against my Showbiz mates and I can tell you they weren't well pleased.'

Mooro often had Kenny playing in matches involving West Ham and he tells a lovely story of the day he and another black guy... West Ham's John Charles... ended up in the bath together.

Kenny had the place in an uproar when he said to John: 'Listen Charlo you've got to move away from me... I keep washing your

Russ Abbott – has more luck keeping goal than with Blackpool's deckchairs!

leg instead of my own!'

Jimmy Tarbuck and Kenny are great mates and in fact are a marvellous double act on stage. They are always game for a laugh at any charity sporting event and in one golf match they paired up to play Sir Matt Busby and Joe Mercer.

Now as all good golfers know the yellow ball markers are the tees of the day at golf courses, while the red balls are the ladies' tees.

Jimmy and Kenny were one up against the soccer greats when old Joe cracked the ball against the red ball marker, smashing it to pieces. As the fourball fell about in laughter Tarby chipped in: 'You're lucky it didn't hit Lynchy Joe... that would have been seven away!'

Kenny as I've mentioned is a close friend of my old china Bobby Moore, who as anyone who knows him will tell you is the most immaculate dresser.

Lynchy like me has had the experience of sharing a room with Bobby and being distracted in the early hours by Mooro meticulously folding every bit of clothing away, in order to look his usual well-turned-out self in the morning.

But on one occasion Kenny had Mooro ready to chase him around the famous Maracana Stadium in Brazil after one of his gags went wrong. Bobby and Kenny had been invited out to Rio by British Caledonian to play in a pro-celebrity golf match and the Brazilians heard that Mooro... a hero in Brazil for his battles with Pele... was in town.

They invited him to present Pele with a flag before a special match between a Pele Brazilian XI and Flamenco.

Bobby didn't want to do it, but Lynchy, as usual willing to try anything once, talked him into it.

'As we walked onto this fabulous pitch the ground was only half full... and there were still around 120,000 people in it,' says Lynchy.

'Suddenly some geezer threw a tomato at me. I chucked it right back and that's when the fun started.

'Suddenly Bobby and I were on the wrong end of all the rotten fruit in Rio, with Mooro, standing there as well-groomed as ever, in cashmere jacket and immaculate flannels, getting the brunt of it.

'We got hit by everything and had to make a run for the dug-out, where we hid for several minutes before a local radio bloke came to our rescue.

'Pele did get his flag, but I know where Mooro would have liked to stick it... but I had my back to the wall!'

One final story from television. It happened during the 1978 World Cup finals in Argentina in that ill-fated Scotland match against Peru.

Hugh Johns was ITV's main commentator at the time and was down to cover the match with the Saint as his co-commentator.

But as often happens abroad the sound line went down and all Hugh's month-long preparations and well-learned pronunciations went out of the window. The network took Arthur Montford's of Scottish Television commentary, but, because Hugh had been billed as commentator in England, Brian Moore back in the London studio announced: 'I'm afraid our scheduled match commentator Hugh Johns has gone missing in Argentina.'

Whereupon Mrs Johns sitting back in Cardiff had the proverbial canary. She got right on the phone to London. What had happened to her husband? Had he been kidnapped by Argentinian bandits or had he met with an accident?

Only a few calming words from a red-faced Brian helped to divert a nervous breakdown!